SALT

SALT

TYPES · USES · RECIPES

with recipes by Valerie Aikman-Smith

RYLAND PETERS & SMALL
LONDON · NEW YORK

Designer Geoff Borin
Senior Editor Abi Waters
Production Manager Gordana Simakovic
Creative Director Leslie Harrington
Editorial Director Julia Charles
Indexer Vanessa Bird

First published in 2024 by Ryland Peters & Small

20–21 Jockey's Fields
London
WC1R 4BW

341 E 116th St,
New York,
NY 10029

www.rylandpeters.com

10 9 8 7 6 5 4 3 2 1

ISBN: 978-1-78879-605-7

Printed in China

A CIP record for this book is available from the British Library. US Library of Congress cataloguing-in-publication data has been applied for.

Notes:

• Both British (Metric) and American (Imperial plus US cups) measurements are included in these recipes for your convenience, however it is important to work with one set of measurements and not alternate between the two within a recipe.

• All spoon measurements are level unless otherwise specified.

• All eggs are medium (UK) or large (US), unless specified as large, in which case US extra-large should be used.

• When a recipe calls for the grated zest of citrus fruit, buy unwaxed fruit.

CONTENTS

SALT,

heavenly salt – every cook's pantry is stocked with it. From everyday cooking salt to the pink rock salt of the Himalayas or the aromatic fleur de sel harvested in Guérande, France, there are flavoured salts, spiced salts, smoked salts and salts of the most beautiful hues. We use this magical ingredient in everything; whether it's for sprinkling over an omelette or decorating the rim of a margarita glass.

We season, preserve, bake, cure, brine, pickle and make rubs with this wonderful ingredient. Harvested from land and sea it comes in a multitude of shapes, textures, colours and tastes. Just a sprinkle of this divine substance can make a dish sing.

Cooks delight in their collections of salts from all over the world. They love to discuss the effects of salt and how they use it to add a freshness and piquancy to food. Some people with a strong devotion to salt even go so far as to carry around a small salt cellar with them.

Salt has been a prized possession since the beginning of civilization. It was once used as a form of currency and wars have been won and lost over it. Nations have been taxed on their salt. In China, salt tax revenues were used to build the Great Wall. The Greeks and the Mayans worshipped their gods with salt offerings. Roman soldiers were given an allowance of salt known as 'salarium', from which the word 'salary' comes. There are salt routes all over the world, which were used to transport salt from continent to continent. In Italy, one of the oldest roads is called Via Salaria, meaning salt route, and Venice has a long history of making herbed salts. At one time salt was so precious it was traded ounce for ounce with gold.

So where does the salt that we buy from our local market come from? It is mined deep in the earth and harvested from salt lakes or salt pans. Salt lakes are naturally occurring inland bodies of water, which are remnants of ancient seas. Salt pans are man-made basins, situated next to the sea, which are flooded with salt waters. These waters evaporate in the sun and the salt that is left behind is harvested.

Wherever it comes from in the world we are always surprised and delighted to have it around.

Remember, if you spill salt, throw a few granules over your shoulder for good luck.

SALT DIRECTORY

ROCK SALT

This is mined from salt deposits deep in the earth and is sometimes coloured with minerals. It has a large grain, which makes it ideal for use when cooking with a salt crust, but otherwise it is usually put in a salt grinder for easier use.

MURRAY RIVER SALT FLAKES

These delicate pink salt flakes come from the Murray River region in Australia. They are harvested from pure underground saline waters rich in minerals, giving it its wonderful taste and pink colour. Good for cooking and used as a pretty garnish.

HIMALAYAN PINK ROCK SALT

This salt is hand-mined in Nepal from ancient salt deposits and is believed to be the purest salt on earth. The iron content gives it its distinct pink colour. Fun to have in a block and grate over food.

GREEN TEA SALT

This salt is made by mixing Matcha, a Japanese green tea powder, with sea salt and grinding it to a fine powder using a pestle and mortar. It adds a gentle taste when sprinkled on salads and is high in amino acids.

SMOKED SALTS

Smoked salts are man-made by smoking the salts with flavoured wood chips. They come in versions such as mesquite or hickory and add a deep flavour to dishes.

HAWAIIAN BLACK LAVA SEA SALT

Crushed black lava and black charcoal are mixed with harvested sea salt to give it its black appearance. It should be sprinkled on food at the last minute. Do not immerse it in liquid as it will lose its colour.

SEA SALT FLAKES

These are large delicate salt crystals made from the evaporation caused by the sun on the sea or salt lakes. Rich in minerals, they come in an array of colours depending on their geographical origin.

HAWAIIAN RED ALAEA SEA SALT

This salt hails from the island of Kauai. 'Alaea' is the name given to the natural mineral found in the run-off from the volcano, which occurs in the rainy season. It is a red clay, which colours the salt pans a deep burnt red colour. This salt is used mostly for garnishing dishes.

SEL GRIS

Sel gris, grey salt, is also known as Celtic sea salt. Hand-harvested from the bottom of the salt flats in Guérande, France, its grey colour comes from the clay in the beds.

JURASSIC SALT

Jurassic salt gets its name from the era 150 million years ago when Utah was mostly under water. When the water dried up, it left behind this mineral-intense salt with a pinkish hue. This salt has a delicate flavour and is perfect for most types of cooking, especially baking.

FLEUR DE SEL

A hand-harvested sea salt
from the Guérande and
Camargue regions of France.
The crystallized salt is
skimmed from the surface
of the salt pans, flooded with
the waters of the Atlantic.
It has a mild flavour.

FLAVOURED SALTS

These salts are made with
fruits, spices (such as saffron),
fresh and dried herbs,
pounded together with salt
using a pestle and mortar.
If you use fresh herbs or fruits,
crush then spread them out
on a baking tray and place
in a low temperature oven
for 30 minutes.

THE SALTED PANTRY

BRINES

Brine is simply salty water, but it can season, flavour and preserve a variety of foods. Remember, once you have brined foods you must throw away the brine; it cannot be used for anything else.

JUNIPER BERRY BRINE

This is when to get out the mortar and pestle and bruise the juniper berries to let those fantastic floral aromas jump out at you. This brine works well with any cut of pork and the flavours soak deep down into the meat.

1 tablespoon juniper berries
4 garlic cloves
4 fresh bay leaves
1 sprig rosemary
130 g/½ cup coarse sea salt
240 ml/1 cup white wine

MAKES 2.2 LITRES/
9 CUPS

In a mortar and pestle, pound the juniper berries, garlic and bay leaves until they are smashed.

Put the juniper berries, garlic and bay into a large saucepan with all the other ingredients, add 2 litres/quarts water and set over a medium-high heat. Bring to the boil and stir until all the salt has dissolved.

Remove from the heat and let cool completely. When the brine has cooled, it is ready to use.

CHILLI BRINE

This brine is excellent for prawns/shrimps in their shells. Only brine seafood for 20 minutes; after that the meat will begin to break up.

Put all the ingredients in a saucepan with 1.5 litres/6¼ cups water and set over a medium-high heat. Bring to the boil and simmer for 5 minutes, stirring until all the salt has dissolved.

Remove from the heat and let cool completely. When the brine has cooled, it is ready to use.

60 g/¼ cup sea salt
2 tablespoons dark brown sugar
6 dried red chillies/chiles
1 tablespoon coriander seeds
4 kaffir lime leaves

MAKES 1.75 LITRES/ 7½ CUPS

SWEET TEA BRINE

Infusing chicken in this sweet tea brine gives the final dish a special taste. Fruity and light, it is the perfect brine for fried chicken.

Put the black tea leaves in a measuring jug/cup and pour over the boiling water. Add the salt, sugar and honey and stir until dissolved. Set aside to cool.

When the brine has cooled completely, it is ready to use.

4 tablespoons black tea leaves
1.5 litres/6¼ cups boiling water
60 g/¼ cup coarse sea salt
3 tablespoons dark brown sugar
60 ml/¼ cup honey

MAKES 1.75 LITRES/ 7½ CUPS

MEDITERRANEAN BRINE

This is not a complicated brine – the flavours are simple so as to
enrich the final dish but not to take over. The rosemary and balsamic
give the brine a Mediterranean touch, which is perfect for all poultry.

65 g/¼ cup coarse sea salt
1 large sprig rosemary
2 garlic cloves
60 ml/¼ cup white balsamic
    vinegar
1 tablespoon black
    peppercorns

MAKES 2.2 LITRES/
9 CUPS

Put all the ingredients in a large saucepan with 2 litres/quarts
water, and set over a medium–high heat. Bring to the boil and
stir until all the salt has dissolved.

Remove from the heat and let cool completely. When the brine
has cooled, it is ready to use.

BEER BRINE FOR THE BARBECUE

Brining ribs and chops really keeps them moist when they hit that fiery
grill. You can leave meats in the brine for 2–3 days; the longer the better.

1 litre/4 cups boiling water
1 bottle Guinness or dark beer
60 g/¼ cup coarse sea salt
3 tablespoons dark brown
    sugar
3 tablespoons molasses
1 tablespoon dried oregano

MAKES 1.5 LITRES/
6½ CUPS

Put all the ingredients in a large bowl, stir until dissolved and set
aside. When the brine has cooled completely, it is ready to use.

ANISE AND APPLE CIDER BRINE

Apple cider gives this brine a kick. If possible, use unfiltered cider as it does make a difference. This is an ideal brine for pork as the apple flavours go together so well. The addition of the anise just adds a little surprise.

Put all the ingredients in a large saucepan and add 2 litres/quarts water. Set the pan over a medium-high heat, bring to the boil and stir until all the salt has dissolved.

Remove from the heat and let cool completely. When the brine has cooled, it is ready to use.

1 tablespoon anise seeds

120 ml/½ cup (hard) apple cider

65 g/¼ cup coarse sea salt

2 garlic cloves, bashed

1 tablespoon black peppercorns

4 fresh bay leaves

MAKES 2.2 LITRES/ 9 CUPS

PRESERVED LEMONS

Added to so many dishes as a refreshing, tangy ingredient or garnish, preserved lemons are essential to the cooking of tagines. Of course, you can buy jars of ready-preserved lemons in Middle Eastern and African stores, as well as some supermarkets and specialist shops, but it is worth making your own. Be as liberal as you like, tossing them in salads and scattering them over your favourite tagines.

10 organic, unwaxed lemons, preferably the small, thin-skinned Meyer variety
120 g/½ cup sea salt
freshly squeezed juice of 3–4 lemons
1 sterilized 1-litre/1-quart glass jar with lid*

MAKES 1 LITRE/QUART

Wash and dry the lemons and slice the ends off each one. Stand each lemon on one end and make two vertical cuts three-quarters of the way through them, as if cutting them into quarters but keeping the base intact.

Stuff 1 tablespoon salt into each lemon and pack them into a large sterilized jar. Seal the jar and store the lemons in a cool place for 3–4 days to soften the skins.

Press the lemons down into the jar, so they are even more tightly packed. Pour the lemon juice over the salted lemons until they are completely covered. Seal the jar again and store it in a cool place for at least 1 month.

Rinse the salt off the preserved lemons before using.

*To sterilize, wash the jar in hot soapy water and rinse. Place in a preheated oven at 160°C fan/180°C/350°F/Gas 4 for 10 minutes.

QUICK PICKLED CUCUMBERS

These crunchy cucumber spears are a snap to make and you can keep them in the fridge for 2 weeks. This is a good basic brining recipe for pickling and you can add other spices depending on what vegetable you are using.

450 g/1 lb. pickling cucumbers
1 tablespoon coarse sea salt
2 teaspoons brown sugar
½ teaspoon black peppercorns
½ teaspoon pink peppercorns
1 teaspoon yellow mustard seeds
4 fresh bay leaves
350 ml/1½ cups apple cider vinegar

1 sterilized 1-litre/1-quart glass jar with lid*

MAKES 1 LITRE/QUART

Cut the cucumbers into spears and pack them into the glass jar.

Put the salt, sugar, peppercorns, mustard seeds, bay leaves, cider vinegar and 60 ml/¼ cup water into a saucepan. Bring to the boil over a medium–high heat, then reduce the heat to medium and simmer until the salt and sugar have dissolved.

Pour the hot pickling juice over the cucumbers, filling the jar to the top. Screw the lid on and allow to cool completely before placing in the refrigerator.

These will keep for up to 2 weeks.

*To sterilize, wash the jar in hot soapy water and rinse. Place in a preheated oven at 160°C fan/180°C/350°F/Gas 4 for 10 minutes.

PRESERVED AUBERGINES IN OIL

Griddling the aubergines/eggplants before preserving will give them a slight smokiness. They will last for 2 weeks in the fridge, but they are certain to be eaten long before then!

Preheat the oven to 120°C fan/140°C/275°F/Gas 1.

Set a colander over a bowl, add the sliced aubergines and sprinkle with the salt. Place a weighted plate on top and leave for 2 hours. Once the time is up, you'll see a pool of brown liquid in the bowl. Discard this, rinse the slices under cold running water, then squeeze them dry with a clean tea towel/dish cloth.

Heat a griddle pan over a high heat until smoking hot, then cook the slices for a few minutes on each side until lightly charred.

Put the vinegar in a saucepan with 450 ml/scant 2 cups cold water and bring to the boil. Once you've got a rolling boil going, drop the aubergine slices in. Cook for 2 minutes, then drain. Arrange the slices on a baking sheet and pop them into the preheated oven for 15 minutes.

Combine the oils and remaining ingredients in the sterilized jar, give it a gentle shake and add the aubergine slices, ensuring they are fully submerged in the oil.

Store in the fridge and eat within 2 weeks.

*To sterilize, wash the jar in hot soapy water and rinse. Place in a preheated oven at 160°C fan/180°C/350°F/Gas 4 for 10 minutes.

2 aubergines/eggplants, cut into 2-cm/¾-inch rounds
50 g/¼ cup coarse sea salt
450 ml/scant 2 cups cider vinegar
150 ml/⅔ cup olive oil
150 ml/⅔ cup sunflower oil
pinch of Greek dried oregano
1 sprig thyme
1 garlic clove, sliced
1 whole dried chilli/chile pepper
1 sterilized 750-ml/3-cup glass jar with a lid*

MAKES 8–10 SERVINGS

PICKLED LIMES

Pickled limes are a great way to jazz up recipes. They're quick and easy to make and are ready in 1 month.

225 g/generous 1 cup sea salt
12 limes, quartered
5 kaffir lime leaves
1 tablespoon pink
    peppercorns
freshly squeezed juice of
    6 limes
1 sterilized 1-litre/1-quart glass
    jar with lid*

MAKES 1 LITRE/QUART

Put 1 tablespoon salt in the sterilized jar and layer with 4 lime quarters. Sprinkle with 2 tablespoons salt, then put 2 kaffir lime leaves and a few peppercorns on top. Continue to layer in this way, packing the limes down firmly as you go, until the jar is full. You may need to push the limes down.

Finish with a layer of salt and pour the lime juice over, to cover the limes. Seal the jar and store in a cool dark place for 1 month before using. Only use the skins of the limes; cut away and discard the pith and flesh.

*To sterilize, wash the jar in hot soapy water and rinse. Place in a preheated oven at 160°C fan/180°C/350°F/Gas 4 for 10 minutes.

SWEET AND SOUR PICKLED ONIONS

500 g/1 lb. 2 oz. pickling
    onions
25 g/2 tablespoons sea salt
1 cinnamon stick
3 small hot red chillies/chiles
2 teaspoons whole black
    peppercorns
70 g/½ cup raisins
200 g/1 cup sugar
375 ml/1½ cups white wine
    vinegar
125 ml/½ cup moscatel or
    sherry vinegar
1 sterilized 1-litre/1-quart glass
    jar with lid*

MAKES 1 LARGE JAR

Pickled onions and gherkins are traditional accompaniments to pâtés and terrines, helping to cut through the richness and, in some cases, fattiness of the dish.

Trim the tops and bottoms off the onions, being careful to keep enough there to hold them together. Prepare an ice-water bath.

Bring a saucepan of water to the boil, then remove from the heat, add the onions and let them sit for 1 minute, then drain. Peel off and discard the skins, then drop the onions straight into the ice-water bath. When all are peeled, drain and transfer to a bowl. Sprinkle with the salt to coat. Cover with a tea towel/dish cloth and leave overnight. The next day rinse the onions and dry on a tea towel, then transfer to a large sterilized jar.

Put the cinnamon, chillies, peppercorns, raisins, sugar and vinegars in a saucepan and bring to the boil, stirring until the sugar has dissolved. Pour the hot liquid and spices over the onions. Seal the jar and leave for at least 2 weeks before serving. These will keep, sealed, for 6 months.

*To sterilize, wash the jar in hot soapy water and rinse. Place in a preheated oven at 160°C fan/180°C/350°F/Gas 4 for 10 minutes.

SPICY KIMCHI

You really can use any fruit or vegetable to make Kimchi. In Korean markets it is most often made with different kinds of cabbage, but you can try chard or kale instead.

1 small Napa cabbage, halved
1 small Savoy cabbage, halved and core removed
150 g/¾ cup sea salt
3 carrots, grated
4 scallions/spring onions, thinly sliced
5-cm/2-inch piece of ginger, peeled and grated
4 radishes, grated
2 Persian cucumbers, grated
120 ml/½ cup rice wine vinegar
2 tablespoons fish sauce
2 tablespoons sambal olek chile paste
1 sterilized 1-litre/1-quart glass jar with lid*

MAKES 1 LITRE/QUART

Cut the cabbages into 2.5-cm/1-inch strips and put in a large ceramic bowl. Dissolve the salt in 1.4 litres/6 cups water and pour over the cabbage. Cover with clingfilm/plastic wrap and let stand at room temperature for 8–24 hours.

Drain the cabbage and return to the bowl with the carrots, spring onions, ginger, radishes and cucumbers. Add the vinegar, fish sauce, sambal olek chile paste and 120 ml/½ cup water and mix.

Spoon the cabbage mixture into the sterilized glass jar and pour over any remaining juice. Screw the lid on tightly and let the jar sit at room temperature for 24 hours.

Refrigerate for at least 5 days before serving. The kimchi will keep in the refrigerator for up to 6 weeks.

*To sterilize, wash the jar in hot soapy water and rinse. Place in a preheated oven at 160°C fan/180°C/350°F/Gas 4 for 10 minutes.

PICCALILLI

Piccalilli is a classic British pickle. Served in pubs alongside a ploughman's lunch or a pork pie, it is a staple condiment that never seems to tire. This wonderful sunny yellow pickle has won a place in people's hearts.

Place the cauliflower, courgettes, shallots, onion and garlic in a large bowl. Sprinkle with the salt, cover and set aside 12–14 hours or overnight.

Rinse the vegetables under cold water and return to the bowl. Place the ginger, cumin, mustard seeds, turmeric, mustard powder, chilli powder, curry powder, cornflour, sugar and vinegar in a pan and bring to the boil over a medium heat. Turn down the heat and stir the mixture continuously for 3–4 minutes until it thickens. Pour over the vegetables and toss to mix thoroughly.

Pack the piccalilli into warm sterilized glass jars, leaving a 5 mm/¼ inch space at the top, and carefully tap the jars on the work surface to get rid of any air pockets. Wipe the jars clean and screw on the lids. Seal the jars for 15 minutes (see below).

Once sealed, store unopened in a cool, dark place for up to 12 months.

*To sterilize, wash the jar in hot soapy water and rinse. Place in a preheated oven at 160°C fan/180°C/350°F/Gas 4 for 10 minutes.

SEALING JARS: Preheat the oven to 100°C fan/120°C/250°F/Gas ½. Pack the fruit or vegetables into sterilized jars leaving space at the top according to the recipe. Screw the lids on, wipe the jars clean and, using jar tongs, place them in an ovenproof baking dish. Seal in the preheated oven for the specified time. Remove the dish from the oven and, using jar tongs, transfer the jars to a cooling rack. Leave undisturbed until they have cooled completely – you will hear a pinging sound as each lids seals. Check to make sure that the centre of the lid is concave. Label and store.

1 large cauliflower, chopped into small florets

3 courgettes/zucchini, finely diced

2 shallots, thinly sliced

1 onion, thinly sliced

3 garlic cloves, finely chopped

65 g salt/¼ cup sea salt

1 tablespoon ground ginger

1 tablespoon ground cumin

1 tablespoon brown mustard seeds

2 tablespoons ground turmeric

2 tablespoons English mustard powder

1 tablespoon chilli/chili powder

1 tablespoon curry powder

3 tablespoons cornflour/cornstarch

100 g/½ cup sugar

600 ml/2½ cups apple cider vinegar

2 sterilized 1-litre/1-quart glass jars with lid*

MAKES 2 LITRES/QUARTS

BUTTERS

Use these delicious salty butters at room temperature. For ease of serving, roll the finished butter into a log by putting the butter mixture on a piece of clingfilm/plastic wrap. Fold the clingfilm over the butter and roll it into a sausage shape. Twist the ends, refrigerate and then, once cold and firm, slice the butter into discs to use.

ANCHOVY BUTTER

115 g/1 stick unsalted butter
4 salted anchovy fillets
30 g/1 oz. chopped
  cornichons
finely grated zest and freshly
  squeezed juice of 1 small
  lemon
cracked black pepper,
  to taste

MAKES 150 G/5½ OZ.

The sharpness of brined cornichons brings out the saltiness of the anchovies in this butter. Perfect for spreading on fresh wholemeal bread.

Put all the ingredients into a food processor and mix until smooth. Refrigerate until ready to use.

INDIAN BUTTER

1 teaspoon each coriander
  seeds and cumin seeds,
  dry-roasted in a small pan
115 g/1 stick unsalted butter
1 garlic clove, chopped
1 teaspoon smoked paprika
1 teaspoon chilli/chili powder
1 teaspoon curry powder
1 teaspoon sea salt
cracked black pepper, to taste

MAKES 140 G/5 OZ.

This butter is excellent spread on naan bread and warmed under the grill, or mix a tablespoon through basmati rice just before serving.

Put all the ingredients into a food processor and mix until smooth. Refrigerate until ready to use.

GREEN PEPPER BUTTER

This is a really simple way of making a quick steak au poivre; just melt a dollop on a grilled steak and let the butter do the rest.

Put all the ingredients into a food processor and mix until smooth. Refrigerate until ready to use.

115 g/1 stick unsalted butter
2 tablespoons brined green peppercorns
sel gris and cracked black pepper, to taste

MAKES 120 G/4½ OZ.

SALTY PEANUT BUTTER

190 g/scant 1½ cups salted
  blistered peanuts
60 ml/¼ cup peanut oil

MAKES 250 G/9 OZ.

Homemade peanut butter is so different from shop-bought. If you can't find old-fashioned blistered peanuts, regular salted peanuts also work well.

Put the peanuts in a food processor. With the motor running, pour in the peanut oil in a steady stream. Process until all the oil has been incorporated and the nuts have been evenly ground.

SMOKED SEA SALT BUTTER

2½ teaspoons smoked sea
  salt
225 g/2 sticks unsalted butter
cracked black pepper

MAKES 250 G/9 OZ.

This is a robust butter, salty and smoky, which lends itself perfectly to grilled meats and vegetables. Spoon some through rice or potatoes just before serving to pack in flavour. Smoked salts are easy to find in your local supermarket.

Put the salt and butter in a food processor and process until smooth. Season with pepper and refrigerate until ready to use.

SMOKED SALT AND THYME BROWN BUTTER

This thyme-infused brown butter can be kept in the freezer for you to slice off a disc when needed.

8 sprigs thyme

100 g/1 stick minus 1 tablespoon unsalted butter

1 teaspoon smoked salt

MAKES 100 G/3½ OZ.

Pull the thyme leaves from their stalks.

Add half the butter to a small saucepan over a medium heat with the thyme leaves and let melt, then bubble, swirling often, until you see lots of brown speckles and the butter has turned into a beurre noisette (brown butter). You want good, brown colour in the pan, but also to avoid burning, so don't walk away. Once it's at beurre noisette stage, remove the pan from the heat, transfer to a bowl and cool down to a lukewarm temperature.

Once ready, gradually add the remaining room temperature butter, whisking to combine. Once the butters and thyme have been incorporated together, add the salt and fold through. Taste to check the seasoning and remember the flavour will mellow slightly when cold, so don't be afraid to be bold!

Leave to cool, then roll into a log in some parchment paper and transfer to the freezer.

When you want some, just chop off a chunk and re-cover the exposed end, to avoid freezer burn. Return to the freezer and use again soon!

DIPS AND RUBS

Dips and rubs are easy to make, often from cupboard ingredients. They brighten up even the dullest slices of bread or cuts of meat.

ANCHOÏADE

55 g/2 oz. anchovy fillets in oil

3 garlic cloves, finely chopped

½ teaspoon herbes de Provence

finely grated zest and freshly squeezed juice of ½ lemon

30 g/scant ¼ cup blanched almonds

2 tablespoons flat-leaf parsley

2 tablespoons olive oil

½ teaspoon fleur de sel

cracked black pepper

SERVES 2

A flavoursome Provençal dip. Spread liberally on toasted baguette slices.

Put all the ingredients, except the pepper, in a food processor and process to a thick paste. Season with cracked black pepper.

BAGNA CAUDA

4 garlic cloves, roughly chopped

120 g/4½ oz. anchovy fillets in oil

finely grated zest of 1 lemon and freshly squeezed juice of ½ lemon

60 ml/¼ cup olive oil

cracked black pepper and sea salt flakes, to taste

SERVES 2

Try dipping an assortment of grilled vegetables into this delicious sauce. Serve with crusty bread.

Mix the garlic and anchovies in a food processor. Transfer to a small pan, add the lemon zest and juice, and warm over a low heat. Gradually mix in the olive oil. Do not let the sauce boil; it should be warmed through. Season to taste.

DUKKAH

A traditional Egyptian dip. You dip a piece of bread into olive oil and then into the dukkah. It also works well as a salty coating for meat and poultry.

In a hot pan, toast the hazelnuts and each of the spices separately. Leave to cool slightly then put all the ingredients in a food processor and pulse a few times.

40g/1½ oz. each hazelnuts, fennel seeds, cumin seeds and coriander seeds

80g/generous ½ cup sesame seeds

1 teaspoon sel gris

½ teaspoon cracked black pepper

MAKES 300 G/10½OZ

MUHAMMARA

115 g/¾ cup walnuts

115 g/generous 2 cups fresh brown breadcrumbs

1 hot red chilli/chile, such as Serrano, chopped

1 garlic clove, roughly chopped

3 tablespoons pomegranate molasses

½ teaspoon ground cumin

½ teaspoon ground coriander

½ teaspoon smoked paprika

125 ml/½ cup walnut oil, plus extra to drizzle

90 g/3 oz. fresh pomegranate seeds

sea salt

handful of mint leaves, to garnish

MAKES 500 G/ 1 LB. 2 OZ.

You can adjust the salt to taste in this refreshing Middle Eastern dip. Serve with flatbreads.

Toast the walnuts in a frying pan/skillet for 2–3 minutes. Leave to cool, then put in a food processor with the other ingredients, reserving one-third of the pomegranate seeds. Process until slightly chunky. Season with sea salt to taste.

Put in a bowl and garnish with the remaining seeds, torn mint leaves and a drizzle of walnut oil.

HARISSA

1 teaspoon cumin seeds

1 teaspoon coriander seeds

3 small red (bell) peppers, roasted until blistering, or shop-bought

3 hot red chillies/chiles, such as Serrano, roughly chopped (including seeds)

1 garlic clove, roughly chopped

½ teaspoon sea salt

60 ml/¼ cup olive oil

MAKES 225 G/8 OZ.

Harissa is a North African chilli/chile purée; use as a flavouring or a rub.

In a small frying pan/skillet, toast the cumin and coriander seeds. Peel the peppers.

Put everything in a food processor and process until smooth.

Store in a glass jar with a tight-fitting lid for up to 2 weeks in the fridge.

SALTED HERBES DE PROVENCE

Makes a great rub for meat or fish.

Mix all the ingredients in a bowl, then store in a glass jar for up to 6 months.

2 tablespoons each dried thyme, dried rosemary, dried basil, fennel seeds, dried sage and Murray River salt flakes

3 tablespoons dried lavender flowers

MAKES 85 G/3 OZ.

SMOKY AFRICAN RUB

This is a simple rub, which is laced with smoked salt, giving a hearty bite. Perfect for a braai, which is the Afrikaans word for barbecue.

Put all the ingredients into an electric spice grinder and process to a coarse powder.

Store the spice mix in a glass jar with a tight-fitting lid for up to 6 months.

1 teaspoon smoked sea salt

1 teaspoon coarse-ground garlic powder

1 teaspoon ground black pepper

1 tablespoon dried chilli flakes/hot red pepper flakes

1 teaspoon fenugreek seeds

2 dried bay leaves

MAKES 3 TABLESPOONS

NIBBLES FOR DRINKS

SALTED PRETZEL BITES

These salty, crunchy, bite-sized morsels are nice served with American mustard. Recipe pictured on page 32.

250 ml/1 cup warm water

2 tablespoons salted butter, in small cubes

3 teaspoons fast-action dried yeast

1 teaspoon white sugar

400 g/3 cups plain/ all-purpose flour, plus extra for dusting

4 teaspoons baking powder

rock salt flakes

American mustard, to serve (optional)

MAKES ABOUT 40

In a glass measuring jug/cup, mix together the warm water, butter, yeast and sugar. Stir until the butter has melted.

Put the flour in a food processor. With the motor running, add the liquid to the flour in a steady stream until all the liquid is incorporated and the dough forms a ball, about 3 minutes. Add a little extra flour if necessary.

Put the dough on a floured worktop and knead for 2 minutes. Form into a ball and put in an oiled bowl. Cover with a tea towel/ kitchen towel and leave to prove in a warm place for 1 hour.

Preheat the oven to 200°C fan/220°C/425°F/Gas 7.

Turn the dough out onto a floured worktop and roll into a 30 x 15-cm/12 x 6-inch rectangle. With a sharp knife, cut 2.5-cm/1-inch strips of dough from the long side. Take these dough strands and cut them into 2.5-cm/1-inch bite-sized pieces. (Alternatively, to make the classic pretzel shape, shape the dough strands into a figure of eight, then continue as below.)

Put the baking powder in a non-stick wok or pan (do not use aluminium) with 1 litre/quart water and bring to the boil. Drop the dough pieces into the water and boil for about 1 minute, then remove with a slotted spoon and place onto non-stick baking sheets. They will puff up. This brining procedure gives the pretzels their slightly hard chewy outside, while the insides remain soft.

Sprinkle the rock salt over the pretzel bites and bake in the preheated oven for 10–15 minutes until brown on top. Serve with American mustard, if desired.

PARMESAN AND SAGE WAFERS

The double whammy of salty Parmesan and Himalayan pink rock salt really packs a punch. These delicate lacy wafers are ideal with a glass of prosecco, or try them instead of croutons on a Caesar salad. Recipe pictured on page 32.

Preheat the oven to 160°C fan/180°C/350°F/Gas 4.

Mix together the Parmesan cheese and sage and season with black pepper. Drop tablespoons of the mixture at 5-cm/2-inch intervals on a non-stick baking sheet. Pat down the mounds with your fingers. Bake in the preheated oven for 5–6 minutes until the mixture is completely melted and the edges are turning golden brown. Keep an eye on them as they brown fast.

Remove the wafers from the oven and set aside for a few moments to firm up. They will be soft when they come out of the oven but will harden as they cool.

With a spatula, carefully remove the wafers and arrange on a wire rack to cool completely. Once cooled, sprinkle with Himalayan pink rock salt

They can be stored in an airtight container for 2 days.

110 g/4 oz. Parmesan cheese, grated
1 tablespoon finely chopped fresh sage
cracked black pepper
Himalayan pink rock salt

MAKES 14

EXTRA-LONG HAWAIIAN BLACK SALTED BREADSTICKS

These breadsticks look stunning sprinkled with black Hawaiian lava sea salt – sea salt blended with volcanic charcoal.

300 ml/1¼ cups warm water
3 tablespoons olive oil
1 tablespoon milk
3 teaspoons fast-action dried yeast
½ teaspoon brown sugar
450 g/scant 3½ cups plain/all-purpose flour, plus extra for dusting
60 ml/¼ cup olive oil
110 g/4 oz. black Hawaiian lava sea salt

MAKES ABOUT 24

In a glass measuring jug/cup mix together the warm water, olive oil, milk, yeast and brown sugar.

Put the flour in a food processor. With the motor running, add the liquid to the flour in a steady stream. Process until all the liquid is incorporated and the dough forms a ball, about 3 minutes.

Transfer the dough to a floured worktop and knead for about 3 minutes. Form into a ball and put in an oiled bowl. Cover with a tea towel/kitchen towel and let prove in a warm place until it doubles in size.

Preheat the oven to 200°C fan/220°C/425°F/Gas 7.

Turn the dough out onto a floured surface and roll it out into a 25 x 40-cm/10 x 16-inch rectangle, about 5 mm/¼ inch thick. Use a sharp knife to cut 1-cm/½-inch strips of dough from the long side of the rectangle. Fold the strips in half and, with the palms of your hands, roll the dough into breadsticks, about 25 cm/10 inches long.

Arrange the breadsticks on non-stick baking sheets, brush with the olive oil and sprinkle with the black Hawaiian lava sea salt.

Bake in the preheated oven for 10 minutes, then turn the sticks over, and bake for another 10 minutes until golden. Leave to cool on a wire rack.

BLACK TRUFFLE POPCORN

Black truffle is one of life's finest luxuries and it lends its rich
flavour to popcorn in the form of black truffle salt. Truffle has been
said to have aphrodisiac properties so be careful who you are with
when you serve it!

In a food processor, blitz the mushrooms to a fine powder and
set aside.

Heat the oil in a large lidded saucepan with a few popcorn
kernels in the pan. When you hear the kernels pop, carefully tip
in the rest of the kernels. Shake the pan over the heat until the
popping stops. Take care when lifting the lid as any unpopped
kernels may still pop from the heat of the pan. Tip the popcorn
into a bowl, removing any unpopped kernels as you go.

Melt the butter in a small saucepan set over a medium heat
and pour over the warm popcorn. Sprinkle over the mushroom
powder and truffle salt, and stir well so that the popcorn is
evenly coated. This popcorn is best served warm.

COOK'S NOTE: If you do not have truffle salt, simply drizzle
a little truffle-infused oil over the popcorn and use regular sea
salt instead.

20 g/¾ oz. dried porcini
    mushrooms
90 g/⅓ cup popcorn kernels
1–2 tablespoons sunflower or
    vegetable oil
70 g/5 tablespoons butter
1 teaspoon black truffle salt

MAKES 1 LARGE BOWL

GOLD POTATO CRISPS WITH TRUFFLE SALT

Potatoes, truffles and salt are a match made in heaven. Use a mandoline to slice the potatoes wafer thin.

500 g/1 lb. 2 oz. Mayan Gold potatoes or similar (about 6 small), skin on
truffle salt
vegetable oil, for deep-frying

SERVES 4–6

Wash and dry the potatoes, slice thinly and set aside.

Heat the oil in the deep-fryer or heavy-bottomed pan until it reaches 180°C (350°F). To test if the oil is hot enough, drop a cube of bread in the oil; it should turn golden brown in about 20 seconds.

Fry the potato slices in batches and drain on paper towels.

Put the drained potato crisps in a bowl, sprinkle with the truffle salt, toss, and serve.

SPICY POPCORN WITH CHILLI SALT

You can't watch a movie without snacks. This popcorn has a fabulous pink tint and chilli/chile kick. Murray River salt comes from the Murray River region in Australia – it has a wonderful taste and pink hue.

4 tablespoons Murray River salt flakes
2 tablespoons chipotle chilli/chili powder, or to taste
2 bags unsalted microwave popcorn

SERVES 4

In a small bowl, mix together the salt and chilli powder.

Cook the popcorn according to the instructions on the packet.

When it has popped, put it in a large bowl, sprinkle with the chilli salt, and toss to mix.

CANDIED SALTED ALMONDS

These spicy, sweet and salty nuts are delicious sprinkled over salads or mixed into a pilaf.

270 g/2 cups raw almonds, skin on
60 g/5 tablespoons dark brown soft sugar
60 g/3 tablespoons maple syrup
1 teaspoon chipotle chilli/chili powder
1 tablespoon sel gris, coarsely ground

MAKES 400 G/14 OZ.

Preheat the oven to 170°C fan/190°C/375°F/Gas 5.

Mix all the ingredients except for the sel gris together in a bowl until the almonds are well coated. Spread out the almonds on a non-stick baking sheet and bake in the preheated oven for 5–8 minutes. The sugars will bubble and turn a darker colour.

Remove the almonds from the oven and stir with a wooden spoon. Sprinkle with sel gris and set aside to cool on the baking sheet before serving. As they cool, the sugars will harden.

The nuts can be stored in an airtight container for a week at room temperature.

SPICED AND MARINATED OLIVES

Salted Marcona almonds bring the salt to this recipe, providing the perfect backdrop to the spiced olives.

1 dried red chilli/chili
90 g/¾ cup Spanish salted Marcona almonds
170 g/1¼ cup green olives
3 kumquats
½ teaspoon cumin seeds
60 ml/¼ cup Spanish olive oil

MAKES 400 G/14 OZ.

Roughly chop the chilli and the almonds and put them in a bowl with the olives.

Thinly slice the kumquats and add to the olive mixture. Sprinkle with cumin seeds, pour over the olive oil and mix thoroughly.

Set aside for at least 1 hour before serving to marinate and let the flavours blend.

CORSICAN FRIED OLIVES

These fried stuffed olives are finished with a sprinkle of fleur de sel, a salt that is harvested from the surface layer of seawater.

In a bowl, mix together the goat's cheese, herbs and orange zest until smooth. Put the mixture in the piping bag and set aside.

Lightly beat the egg in a small bowl and set aside. Put the flour on a small plate and the breadcrumbs on another.

Using the piping bag, pipe each olive full with the cheese mixture. Dip each olive in the flour, then the egg, and toss in the breadcrumbs until well coated.

Heat the oil in a heavy-bottomed pan until the oil reaches 180°C (350°F). Test the oil by dropping in a cube of bread; it should turn golden brown in about 20 seconds.

Fry the olives in batches until crispy and golden brown, about 1 minute. Drain on kitchen paper/paper towels.

Sprinkle generously with the fleur de sel and serve.

115 g/4 oz. goat's cheese, at room temperature
1 teaspoon herbes de Provence
finely grated zest of 1 orange
1 egg
1 tablespoon plain/ all-purpose flour
60 g/1½ cups panko or coarse breadcrumbs
40 large green and black stoned/pitted olives
fleur de sel
vegetable oil, for deep-frying
piping/pastry bag with a small nozzle/tip

MAKES 40

ROASTED SWEET POTATO WEDGES WITH HAWAIIAN ALAEA SEA SALT

This is a pretty dish to look at, as well as being very tasty. The beautiful orange flesh and dark red skins of the sweet potatoes are offset by the ochre-coloured salt. Hawaiian red alaea sea salt is a garnishing salt only, rich in minerals, which give it such a vivid colour. When cooked, it loses both its colour and flavour.

900 g/2 lb. sweet potatoes (about 3), skin on
60 ml/¼ cup olive oil
cracked black pepper
Hawaiian red alaea sea salt
Goat's Cheese Dip with Citrus Salt (see page 46), to serve

SERVES 4

Preheat the oven to 170°C fan/190°C/375°F/Gas 5.

Rinse and dry the sweet potatoes. Cut them into thick wedges and arrange on a non-stick baking sheet. Pour the olive oil over them, tossing the wedges to make sure they are evenly coated. Season with cracked black pepper.

Bake in the preheated oven for 10 minutes. Turn the wedges over and return to the oven for another 10–15 minutes, until golden brown and crispy on the edges. Pierce the wedges with a sharp knife to make sure they are cooked through.

Remove from the oven, sprinkle generously with Hawaiian red alaea sea salt, and serve with the Goat's Cheese Dip.

GOAT'S CHEESE DIP WITH CITRUS SALT

I love this goats' milk yoghurt dip. It is perfect as a light snack in warm weather, served with pitta, cut raw vegetables or the sweet potato wedges on page 44. Recipe pictured on page 45.

900 g/2 lb. goat's milk yogurt, preferably organic

extra-virgin olive oil

CITRUS SALT

finely grated zest of 1 lemon

2 tablespoons rock salt

muslin/cheesecloth square

MAKES 1 KG/2 LB. 4 OZ.

Line a sieve/strainer with the muslin square. You can also use a single layer of kitchen paper/paper towel or a coffee filter.

Rest the lined sieve on the rim of a bowl deep enough to catch the drained fluid. Empty the goat's milk yogurt into the lined sieve, cover with clingfilm/plastic wrap and leave in the refrigerator overnight.

Make the citrus salt by pounding the lemon zest and salt in a pestle and mortar. Transfer to a small bowl.

The next day, remove the goat's cheese from the refrigerator and discard the liquid. To serve, put the cheese in a serving bowl. Drizzle with olive oil and sprinkle with the citrus salt.

PADRON PEPPERS

One in every dozen Padron peppers has a fiery hit, so be prepared with a glass of cold beer to hand.

Put a sauté pan over a high heat. When it starts to smoke, turn the heat down to medium. Add the olive oil and swirl the pan once to cover the bottom with oil.

Add the peppers and cook until slightly blistered, stirring occasionally. Empty the hot peppers into a bowl and sprinkle generously with the sel gris.

60 ml/¼ cup olive oil
450 g/1 lb. Padron peppers
sel gris

SERVES 4–6

MATCHSTICK FRIES WITH SICHUAN PEPPER SALT

Super-skinny and delicate, matchsticks are an upmarket version of fries, so serve them for your next special meal. They're especially nice as a nibble with drinks or served with venison or very good steak.

2 large floury potatoes, roughly the same size
cornflour/cornstarch, for dusting
vegetable or sunflower oil, for deep-frying

SICHUAN PEPPER SALT

1 tablespoon Sichuan peppercorns
2 tablespoons coarse rock salt

SERVES 4 AS A SIDE

For the Sichuan pepper salt, heat the peppercorns in a small frying pan/skillet until hot but not smoking. Transfer to a plate to cool. Combine with the salt and grind in a spice mill or with a pestle and mortar. Set aside.

Peel the potatoes and trim on all sides to get a block. Cut the block into thin slices, then cut the slices thinly into matchsticks.

Put the potatoes into a bowl of iced water for at least 5 minutes, to remove excess starch and prevent sticking when frying. Put the cornflour in a shallow bowl.

Fill a large saucepan one-third full with the oil or, if using a deep-fryer, follow the manufacturer's instructions. Heat the oil to 190°C (375°F). Test the oil by dropping in a cube of bread; it should turn golden brown in about 20 seconds.

Drain the potatoes and dry very well, then toss to coat lightly with the cornflour. Put in a sieve/strainer to help shake off any excess cornflour.

Working in batches, fry about a handful of potatoes at a time. Place the potatoes in a frying basket and lower into the hot oil carefully. Fry for about 5 minutes, then remove and drain on kitchen paper/paper towels. Repeat until all of the potatoes have been fried.

Sprinkle with the Sichuan pepper salt and serve.

SMALL PLATES AND APPETIZERS

SALT AND PEPPER SQUID WITH SANSHO SPICY DIP

This recipe, using spicy, citrusy Sansho pepper, is a spin on the ever-popular salt and pepper prawns/shrimp served in Chinese restaurants around the world. Dip the freshly fried squid into the spiced mayo and enjoy.

½ teaspoon ground Sansho pepper
2 teaspoons sea salt
65 g/½ cup rice flour
450 g/1 lb. squid, cleaned and sliced
freshly squeezed juice of 1 lemon
vegetable oil, for deep-frying

SANSHO SPICY DIP

115 g/½ cup good-quality mayonnaise
5 g/¼ cup Vietnamese or regular basil leaves, finely chopped, plus extra leaves to serve
½ teaspoon ground Sansho pepper
½ teaspoon sea salt
grated zest of 1 lemon

SERVES 4

To make the dip, whisk all the ingredients together in a small bowl until well combined. Set aside.

In a large shallow bowl mix together the Sansho pepper, salt and rice flour. Put the squid in another bowl and pour the lemon juice over the squid.

Pour enough oil into a large saucepan to come halfway up the sides, then place the pan over a medium–high heat until the oil starts to simmer.

Take a few pieces of squid at a time and toss in the flour mixture to coat. Working in batches, deep fry for 2–3 minutes until golden and cooked through. Transfer to a wire rack to drain.

Pile the cooked squid in a shallow bowl, add a few extra basil leaves and serve with the dip.

HOME-CURED ANCHOVIES

Throughout the Mediterranean it is the cheap, small fish that form a major part of the staple diet. Abundant in the Mediterranean sea and full of healthy fats, anchovies are delicious once cured. Smoked sea salt is used to cure these, but regular sea salt will work, too.

Fillet the anchovies or sprats, discarding the heads, bones and guts (or ask your fishmonger to do this for you).

Scatter one-quarter of the salt on a plate that won't react with the salt (ceramic, glass, plastic or stainless steel). Layer the fillets on top, salting between each layer. These don't need to be fully encased in salt, so you should have enough, but use a little more if you feel you need to. Cover and refrigerate for 6 hours.

Put the sherry vinegar and lemon juice in a small bowl and whisk to combine. Remove the anchovies from the fridge, rinse the salt off them and pat them dry with kitchen paper/paper towels. Put them in a shallow dish and pour over the sherry vinegar mixture. Shuffle them around to ensure they are all submerged, cover and let them pickle in the fridge for 1 hour. Remove them from the pickling liquor, shaking off some of the excess.

Add the lemon zest, garlic, bay leaves and oregano to your jar. Add the cured fillets and pour in the olive oil to cover. These are best eaten after a day or two so that they have time to soak in the flavours, but refrigerate them until ready to serve and eat within 3 days.

To serve, lay anchovies out flat on a plate, leave for 10 minutes to take the fridge chill off and drizzle with some of the oil from the jar (if the oil has solidified, just leave 1–2 tablespoon of it to liquify at room temperature) and scatter over some crushed pink peppercorns (if using). Add a few lemon wedges for squeezing and serve with rustic bread and a glass of chilled white wine.

*To sterilize, wash the jar in hot soapy water and rinse. Place in a preheated oven at 160°C fan/180°C/350°F/Gas 4 for 10 minutes.

12 fresh anchovies or sprats
about 50 g/¼ cup coarse smoked sea salt or coarse sea salt
100 ml/generous ⅓ cup sherry vinegar
freshly squeezed juice of 1 lemon
5-cm/2-inch piece of lemon zest
1 garlic clove, thickly sliced
2 dried bay leaves
pinch of Greek dried oregano
250 ml/1 cup light olive oil
a few pink peppercorns, crushed, to garnish (optional)
lemon wedges, for squeezing
chunks of rustic bread, to serve
1 sterilized 750-ml/3-cup glass jar with a lid*

MAKES 8 SERVINGS

SALT COD BRANDADE

A wonderful French Mediterranean dish, this can be a simple lunch on its own, served as an appetizer before a larger meal, or even as part of a banquet of smaller dishes. Brandade can be made without the potatoes for a cleaner flavour, but they do add a delicious creaminess to the dish.

500 g/1 lb. 2 oz. cod fillet, skinned and boned
1 brown onion, finely chopped
4 garlic cloves, thinly sliced
200 g/7 oz. Maris Piper potatoes, peeled and diced
200 ml/generous ¾ cup whole milk
100 ml/generous ⅓ cup olive oil, plus extra for drizzling
100 ml/generous ⅓ cup double/heavy cream
1 baguette, sliced diagonally into 5-mm/¼-inch slices
sea salt and freshly ground black pepper

SALAD

1 cucumber, peeled and finely chopped
small bunch of dill, thinly sliced
1 small fennel bulb, thinly sliced
grated zest and freshly squeezed juice of 1 lemon

SERVES 8-10

Begin by making the salad. Toss the cucumber, dill, fennel and lemon zest and juice together in a large mixing bowl. Set aside for at least 1 hour in advance so the flavours can combine and to mute the fennel slightly.

Generously season the cod fillet with salt on both sides, cover and set in the fridge for at least 24 hours.

Rinse and pat dry, then put the cod fillet, onion, garlic, potatoes and milk in a saucepan set over a gentle heat. Bring to a low simmer and cook for 20 minutes; check the potatoes are fully cooked, then strain off any excess milk.

While still hot, transfer the mixture to a food processor and blend. With the motor running, slowly pour in the oil and double cream. You should now have a thick paste.

Toast the bread slices under a medium grill/broiler until golden.

Serve the brandade, drizzled with oil and sprinkled with black pepper, alongside the salad and toasts.

ITALIAN-STYLE FLATBREAD WITH PUTTANESCA TOPPING

This recipe makes use of two French salts: sel gris and fleur de sel. These both come from the Guérande region of France.

To make the dough, mix the flour, chilli flakes and sel gris in a food processor. Pour the warm water into a measuring jug/cup and add the olive oil, yeast and brown sugar. Add the liquid to the flour mixture in a steady stream. Process for 3 minutes until the liquid is incorporated and the dough forms a ball.

Transfer the dough to a floured worktop and knead for about 3 minutes. Form into a ball and put in an oiled bowl. Cover and prove in a warm place until it doubles in size.

To make the topping, mix all of the ingredients, except the anchovies and seasoning, in a bowl.

Preheat the oven to 220°C fan/240°C/475°F/Gas 9.

Roll the dough into a long oval and place on a baking sheet. Prick it all over with a fork, brush with olive oil and top with the puttanesca topping. Arrange the anchovies on top and season with fleur de sel and cracked black pepper.

Bake the bread for around 15 minutes until the dough is crisped. Sprinkle with the fresh basil and parsley, add some more salt pepper, and drizzle with extra olive oil.

225 g/1¾ cups plain/
    all-purpose flour, plus extra
    for dusting
1 teaspoon red chilli flakes/
    hot red pepper flakes
1 teaspoon sel gris
150 ml/⅔ cup warm water
2 tablespoons olive oil, plus
    extra for brushing and
    drizzling
1½ teaspoons fast-action
    dried yeast
¼ teaspoon brown sugar
2 tablespoons basil
2 tablespoons flat leaf parsley

PUTTANESCA TOPPING

12 small cured black olives,
    stoned/pitted
150 g/5½ oz. cherry tomatoes
2 garlic cloves, finely chopped
1 tablespoon small salted
    capers
¼ small red onion, thinly
    sliced
1 teaspoon dried oregano
3 tablespoons olive oil
8 anchovy fillets
fleur de sel and cracked
    black pepper

SERVES 4

OLIVE SUPPLI

Traditional supplì contain mozzarella and are known in Rome as
supplì al telefono, as when you bite into them the cheese stretches
like a telephone wire. This version hides a salty black olive instead.

17 cured black olives, stoned/
   pitted
40 g/generous ¼ cup plain/
   all-purpose flour
2 eggs, beaten
140 g/2 cups breadcrumbs
saffron salt
vegetable oil, for deep-frying

RISOTTO

20 g/¾ oz. dried porcini
   mushrooms
250 ml/1 cup white wine
500 ml/2 cups chicken stock
2 tablespoons olive oil
1 garlic clove, finely chopped
2 tablespoons thyme leaves
1 tablespoon chopped
   rosemary
200 g/generous 1 cup arborio
   rice
60 g/2 oz. Parmesan cheese,
   grated
sea salt and cracked black
   pepper

MAKES 17

For the risotto, soak the mushrooms in the wine for 30 minutes. Drain, reserving the liquid, and chop roughly. Pour the reserved liquid into a small pan with the chicken stock. Bring to the boil and reduce to a simmer.

Put the olive oil, garlic, thyme, rosemary and mushrooms in a medium pan and cook over a medium-high heat for a few seconds, coating with the olive oil. Add the rice and stir for 2–3 minutes until well coated and translucent. Start adding the stock, a ladleful at a time, stirring continuously until the liquid has been absorbed. Continue until you have used all the liquid, about 20 minutes.

Stir in the cheese and season with sea salt and cracked black pepper. Pour onto a large plate and spread out to cool.

To make the supplì, take tablespoons of cooled risotto and form 17 balls. With your forefinger make a dent in each risotto ball and place an olive in the centre. Roll the risotto ball in your hand to reshape and cover the olive.

Dust the supplì balls with flour, dip into the beaten egg, and then toss in the breadcrumbs until coated. At this stage they can be left to rest in the refrigerator for up to 6 hours before cooking.

Heat the oil in a heavy-bottomed pan until the oil reaches 180°C (350°F). Test the oil by dropping in a cube of bread; it should turn golden brown in about 20 seconds.

Fry the supplì in batches until crispy and golden brown, about 2 minutes. Drain on kitchen paper/paper towels.

Sprinkle generously with saffron salt and serve.

SALT COD LATKES WITH GREEN OLIVE SALSA

Here is a fun spin on bacalhau, the famous Portuguese salt cod fritters, with a rich green olive salsa to pile on top. Look for green olives marinated in herbs; they have a deep earthy flavour and, when combined with the latkes, bring all the flavours of the Mediterranean together. When buying the salt cod, make sure the flesh is pure white.

Put the salt cod in a bowl and cover with cold water. Place in the refrigerator for 2 days, changing the water four times a day. This will rehydrate the cod and remove any excess salt.

When the cod is ready, drain, put in a pan and cover with cold water. Bring to the boil and cook for 15 minutes until the cod begins to break away from the skin and bones. Remove from the heat, drain and cool. Using a fork, flake the fish, discarding the skin and bones. Mash and set aside.

Peel and roughly grate the potatoes. In a large bowl mix together the cod, potatoes, oregano, spring onions, garlic and egg. Season with black pepper and set the latke mixture aside.

To make the salsa, roughly chop the herbed green olives and put in a small bowl. Add the lemon zest along with the olive oil and mix thoroughly.

Heat a medium-sized non-stick sauté pan over a medium–high heat and drizzle with enough olive oil to fry the latkes. Drop heaped tablespoons of the latke mixture into the sauté pan.

Cook the latkes in batches for 2–3 minutes on each side until crispy and golden brown and the potato is cooked.

Arrange the latkes on a serving plate, top with a little salsa and serve.

500 g/1 lb. 2 oz. salt cod
500 g/1 lb. 2 oz. russet potatoes, or similar starchy potatoes
2 tablespoons oregano leaves, roughly chopped
2 tablespoons spring onions/ scallions, chopped
1 garlic clove, finely chopped
1 egg, lightly beaten
cracked black pepper
olive oil, for frying

GREEN OLIVE SALSA

12 herbed green olives such as Picholine, stoned/pitted
1 tablespoon finely grated lemon zest
2 tablespoons olive oil

MAKES 24

GAZPACHO WITH SMOKED SALTED CROUTONS

Gazpacho is lovely made with heirloom tomatoes of different colours, but if you can't find them, use any very ripe and tasty tomatoes. The sherry vinegar is the key to gazpacho, so seek out a heady one from Jerez in Spain – it will make all the difference.

1.3 kg/3 lb. heirloom tomatoes
1 garlic clove
1 small red onion
2 Persian cucumbers
1 green (bell) pepper
1 Serrano chilli/chile
    (red or green)
60 ml/¼ cup extra virgin olive
    oil, plus extra to serve
60 ml/¼ cup Jerez sherry
    vinegar
sel gris and cracked black
    pepper

SMOKED SALTED
CROUTONS

1 small baguette
1 garlic clove, finely chopped
60 ml/¼ cup olive oil
1 tablespoon smoked sea salt

SERVES 4

To peel the tomatoes, fill a small bowl with ice and water and set aside. Bring a medium-sized saucepan of water to the boil. Using a sharp knife, score a cross in the top of each tomato. Drop the tomatoes into the hot water for 30 seconds. Remove with a slotted spoon and drop into the iced water for 1 minute. Remove from the water and peel. Cut the tomatoes in halves or quarters, depending on the size, and put in the food processor.

Roughly chop the garlic, onion and cucumbers, then add to the tomatoes. Cut the green pepper and Serrano chilli in half and remove the white pith and seeds. Chop and add to the tomatoes. Pulse the tomato mixture until it is chunky. Pour the gazpacho into a large bowl and stir in the olive oil and Jerez sherry vinegar. Chill in the refrigerator until ready to serve.

Preheat the oven to 180°C fan/200°C/400°F/Gas 6.

To make the croutons, slice the baguette lengthways into four slices and lay the slices on a baking sheet. Mix the garlic and olive oil in a small bowl and drizzle over the bread. Sprinkle with the smoked sea salt and bake in the preheated oven for about 8–10 minutes until golden.

Pour the gazpacho into four bowls, season with the sel gris and cracked black pepper and drizzle each bowl with a little olive oil. Serve with the smoked salted croutons.

SALT-CRUSTED CITRUS PRAWNS WITH CHILLI DIPPING SAUCE

This is a showstopper at any dinner party. Crack open the salt crust at the table and let your guests be dazzled by the heavenly aromas and the bright pink shells.

Preheat the oven to 220°C fan/240°C/475°F/Gas 9.

In a large bowl mix together the lime zest and juice, salt and 250 ml/1 cup water. The mixture should be the consistency of wet sand. Spread a layer of the salt mixture in a baking dish and arrange the prawns on top. Cover with the remaining salt mixture and pat well down, making sure the prawns are completely covered and there are no gaps anywhere.

Bake in the preheated oven for 15 minutes. The salt should be slightly golden on top.

Whisk together all the dipping sauce ingredients until the sugar has dissolved. Divide among four small bowls.

When the prawns are ready, take them out of the oven and leave them to rest for 5 minutes. Using the back of a knife, crack open the crust and remove the top part. Serve at the table.

Let guests help themselves, peel their own prawns and dip in the chilli sauce. Have a large empty bowl handy for the shells.

finely grated zest and freshly squeezed juice of 2 limes
1.8 kg/4 lb. coarse sea salt
450 g/1 lb. large raw prawns/ jumbo shrimp, such as tiger prawns, unshelled

CHILLI DIPPING SAUCE

2 red chillies/chiles, finely chopped
4 kaffir lime leaves, finely shredded
1 spring onion/scallion, finely chopped
1 garlic clove, finely chopped
125 ml/½ cup fish sauce
finely grated zest and freshly squeezed juice of 2 limes
1 tablespoon rice wine vinegar
1 tablespoon brown sugar
1 tablespoon peanuts, chopped

SERVES 4

GRAVADLAX

It seems everyone has a favourite way of making this classic. This overnight version is quick compared with the traditional method of curing for several days. Wild salmon makes a huge difference; if it's not available, use organic farmed salmon. It will keep for 5 days in the refrigerator. Serve with lemon wedges and crusty bread.

2 tablespoons juniper berries

2 tablespoons black peppercorns, crushed

110 g/4 oz. coarse sea salt

225 g/generous 1 cup brown sugar

3 bunches of dill

1.1-kg/2 lb. 4-oz. wild salmon fillet, boned and with skin on (this is 1 side of a whole salmon)

60 ml/¼ cup gin

lemon wedges, to serve

CAPER SAUCE

225 g/8 oz. crème fraîche

2 tablespoons sea salt

2 tablespoons cornichons

1 tablespoon salted capers

finely grated zest and freshly squeezed juice of 1 lemon

SERVES 8

You will need a baking sheet or shallow dish that will accommodate the salmon. Line the bottom of this with clingfilm/plastic wrap.

Crush the juniper berries and black peppercorns using a pestle and mortar.

In a bowl, mix together the salt and brown sugar, along with the crushed peppercorns and juniper berries. Sprinkle half the salt mixture on top of the prepared baking sheet or dish and spread 1 bunch of dill over the salt mixture. Place the salmon, skin-side down, on top of the dill and drizzle with the gin. Cover the salmon with the remainder of the salt mixture and then top with the remaining dill.

Cover the salmon with clingfilm, making sure it is airtight. Next, you need to put a weight on the salmon; a heavy saucepan or pizza stone is ideal. Put the salmon in the refrigerator overnight to cure for about 12 hours.

To make the caper sauce, put all the ingredients in a food processor and pulse until roughly chopped. Transfer to a bowl, cover and refrigerate.

Unwrap the salmon fillet and remove the dill. Place the salmon on a wooden board. Using the back of a knife, scrape off the salt mixture.

To serve, cut the salmon in diagonal slices as thinly as possible. Serve with the caper sauce.

MAIN MEALS

MISO AND NUT-CRUSTED SALMON

Miso is a traditional staple of Japanese cooking. It is made by fermenting soya beans in sea salt, which results in a thick paste. Most common are white, yellow and red miso. The delicate, slightly salty and fruity flavour of yellow miso really enhances the flavour of wild salmon. This is a fantastic easy supper dish and healthy, too.

2 wild salmon fillets, centre cut, about 225 g/8 oz. each
1 tablespoon olive oil
chopped chives, to garnish
lemon wedges, to serve

MISO AND NUT TOPPING

1 tablespoon yellow miso paste
60 g/½ cup cashews, roughly chopped
½ red Serrano chilli/chile, finely chopped
finely grated zest and freshly squeezed juice of 1 lime
1 tablespoon toasted sesame oil

SERVES 2

Preheat the oven to 180°C fan/200°C/400°F/Gas 6.

Rinse and dry the salmon. Drizzle the olive oil into a small baking dish and place the salmon fillets in it.

To make the topping, mix together the miso, cashews, chilli, lime zest and juice and sesame oil. Divide the mixture and spread on top of the salmon fillets.

Cook in the preheated oven for 12–15 minutes until the fish is cooked and the topping is golden brown.

Garnish with chopped chives and serve with lemon wedges.

SALT-CRUSTED SEA BASS

Sea bass is also known as branzino. It is a white flaky fish with a sweetish taste. You could use any firm fish for this recipe. The fennel seeds in the salt crust add an extra layer of flavour.

Preheat the oven to 200°C fan/220°C/425°F/Gas 7.

Wash the fish and pat dry. Stuff the fish with the rosemary, lemon slices, fennel and garlic. Drizzle with the white wine.

In a large bowl, lightly whisk the egg whites. Add the salt and fennel seeds and mix until it is the consistency of wet sand. Spread half the salt mixture in the bottom of a baking dish and lay the fish on top. Season with cracked black pepper. Cover the fish with the remainder of the salt and pack tightly, making sure there are no holes for the steam to escape.

Bake in the preheated oven for 30 minutes, then remove and leave the fish to rest untouched for another 5 minutes.

Crack open the salt crust with the back of a knife and remove the salt from around the fish. Serve with lemon wedges.

1 whole sea bass, about 900 g/2 lb., cleaned
2 sprigs rosemary
1 lemon, sliced
½ fennel bulb, thinly sliced
1 garlic clove, thinly sliced
60 ml/¼ cup white wine
5 egg whites
1.4 kg/3 lb. coarse sea salt or rock salt
4 tablespoons fennel seeds
cracked black pepper
lemon wedges, to serve

SERVES 2

HOME-SALTED COD WITH CHORIZO AND POTATOES

For centuries fish has been salted to preserve it for the winter. Salt cod is popular in many regions of the world, including Spain where this dish has its origins. Rather than using ready salted cod (which needs 24 hours' pre-soaking before use) here you salt your own fish for just a couple of hours. It is much fresher tasting and far less salty.

4 cod fillets, about 180 g/
  6½ oz. each
50 g/1¾ oz. sea salt
2 tablespoons extra virgin
  olive oil
50 g/1¾ oz. chorizo, diced
500 g/1 lb. 2 oz. potatoes
  (any variety), peeled and
  thickly sliced
6 plum tomatoes, peeled
  and chopped
1 garlic clove, finely chopped
4 sprigs thyme
50 g/3½ tablespoons
  unsalted butter, diced
12 stoned/pitted black olives
1 tablespoon freshly squeezed
  lemon juice
¼ bunch of flat-leaf parsley,
  chopped
sea salt and cracked black
  pepper
aïoli (see right), to serve

SERVES 4

Put the cod fillets in a ziplock bag and add the salt. Seal the bag and give it a good shake to evenly distribute the salt. Set aside for 2 hours, then remove the fillets from the bag and wash off all the salt. Soak the cod in cold water for 15 minutes, then dry thoroughly on kitchen paper/paper towels.

Heat the oil in a large casserole and fry the chorizo over a medium heat for 2–3 minutes until golden and the oil is red. Remove with a slotted spoon and set aside. Add the potatoes to the pan and cook over a high heat for 5 minutes until evenly browned. Return the chorizo to the pan, along with the tomatoes, garlic and thyme. Season with salt and pepper.

Bring the sauce to the boil, then cover and simmer over a low heat for 20 minutes. Remove the lid, place the cod fillets in the sauce, and then top them with the butter. Add the olives and lemon juice, cover and simmer for a further 10 minutes until the fish is cooked through. Scatter with parsley and serve with aïoli.

AÏOLI: Place 2 egg yolks, 2 teaspoons freshly squeezed lemon juice or white wine vinegar, 2 teaspoons Dijon mustard and a little salt into a bowl and whisk until frothy. Very gradually add 200 ml/generous ¾ cup olive oil (or a mixture of extra virgin olive oil and sunflower oil), whisking continuously until the sauce is thick and glossy. Season to taste.

CRISPY ROAST DUCK WITH ASIAN GREENS

Rubbing salt over the duck draws excess moisture out of the skin, while scalding makes for a crispy skin when roasted.

Wash and dry the duck. Rub the salt all over the duck skin, cover and leave in the refrigerator overnight.

Put the roasting rack on the lined roasting tin. Bring a kettle of water to the boil. Put the duck in a large bowl and pour boiling water over it. Immediately remove the duck from the bowl and place on the roasting rack in the roasting tin. Set aside.

Preheat the oven to 180°C fan/200°C/400°F/Gas 6.

Stuff the duck with the orange halves. Mix all the honey glaze ingredients together in a bowl and brush over the duck. Roast in the preheated oven for 30 minutes, remove from the oven, and drain off the fat that has accumulated in the bottom of the pan. You may need to cover the tips of the wings with foil, as they will be very crispy. Turn the oven down to 170°C fan/190°C/375°F/Gas 5 and put the duck back in the oven for another 30 minutes.

Remove the duck from the oven and leave it to rest for about 15 minutes in a warm place.

To prepare the Asian greens, whisk the peanut oil, sesame oil, red wine vinegar, soy sauce and honey together. Season with the cracked black pepper and green tea salt. Put the salad greens in a bowl and toss with the dressing.

Carve the duck and serve with the salad.

1 duck, about 1.4 kg/3 lb.
3 tablespoons coarse sea salt

HONEY GLAZE

4 star anise, crushed
100 ml/generous ⅓ cup honey
1 teaspoon ground cinnamon
finely grated zest of 1 orange and freshly squeezed juice of ½ orange (reserve both halves for stuffing the duck)
1 teaspoon crushed Sichuan peppercorns
2 tablespoons soy sauce
2.5-cm/1-inch piece of fresh ginger, grated
2 red Thai chillies/chiles, chopped
2 tablespoons dark brown sugar

ASIAN GREENS

3 tablespoons peanut oil
2 tablespoons toasted sesame oil
2 tablespoons red wine vinegar
1 teaspoon soy sauce
1 teaspoon honey
350 g/12 oz. salad greens
green tea salt and cracked black pepper

roasting rack
roasting tin lined with foil

SERVES 4

JASMINE-BRINED ROASTED POUSSINS WITH SALSA VERDE

Brining the poussins ensures a crispy skin when roasted. You can use any tea to make the brine, but jasmine tea infuses a floral taste into the poussins and creates a subtle flavour when cooked. You can also make this with Cornish game hen.

2 poussins weighing 700 g/
  1½ lb. (or 1 Cornish game
  hen)
1 small unwaxed lemon
1 garlic clove, crushed
1 tablespoon olive oil
sea salt and cracked black
  pepper

BRINE

4 tablespoons jasmine tea
  or 4 jasmine teabags
1.5 litres/quarts boiling water
60 g/2 oz. coarse rock salt
1 tablespoon dark brown
  sugar

SALSA VERDE

20 g/1 packed cup flat-leaf
  parsley leaves
20 g/1 packed cup coriander
  leaves
20 g/1 packed cup mint
  leaves
2 garlic cloves, finely chopped
1 tablespoon brined capers
125 ml/½ cup olive oil

SERVES 2

First make the brine. Put the jasmine tea in a large measuring jug/cup and pour over the boiling water. Add the salt and sugar and stir until dissolved. Set aside to cool completely.

Wash and dry the poussins and put in a deep dish. Pour the cooled brine over them, cover and refrigerate for 6–8 hours.

When you are ready to cook, preheat the oven to 170°C fan/ 190°C/375°F/Gas 5. Remove the poussins from the brine and pat dry, removing any leftover tea leaves. Discard the brining mixture; it cannot be used again.

Place the poussins in a roasting tin. Zest the lemon and set the zest aside for the salsa verde. Cut the lemon into quarters and stuff the cavity with them. Tie the legs together with kitchen string/twine. Mix together the garlic and oil and rub over the skin of the poussins. Season with sea salt and cracked black pepper.

Roast in the preheated oven for 35 minutes until cooked and the poussin juices run clear.

To make the salsa verde, put the reserved lemon zest in a food processor with all the salsa ingredients and pulse until roughly chopped. Be careful not to overprocess; you want the salsa to be slightly chunky. Season with sea salt and black pepper.

When the poussins are ready, remove from the oven and set aside to rest for 10 minutes, covered with aluminium foil, in a warm place. Carve and serve with the salsa verde.

MUSTARD AND HERB CHICKEN BAKED IN A SALT CRUST

This chicken dish is so easy to prepare. You will be amazed at how beautifully succulent it is, as the salt crust keeps all the moisture in during cooking. As you are using egg whites to help bind the salt, you can save the yolks and make some aïoli (see page 76) to go with the cold leftovers.

Preheat the oven to 170°C fan/190°C/375°F/Gas 5.

Stuff the chicken with the lemon halves and rub the mustard all over the skin. Sprinkle with the herbes de Provence and season with cracked black pepper. Set the chicken aside.

In a large bowl lightly beat the egg whites until frothy. Add the salt and mix thoroughly. The mixture should be the consistency of wet sand.

Spread a thin layer of salt evenly on the bottom of a roasting tin or baking dish. Put the chicken on top and cover with the rest of the salt mixture. Pat down well and make sure there are no holes from which the steam can escape.

Bake the chicken in the preheated oven for 1 hour. You'll notice that the salt will turn a golden brown. Remove the chicken from the oven and leave it to rest for 10 minutes.

Using the back of a knife, crack open the crust and remove. Put the chicken on a wooden board and carve.

1 chicken, about 1.5–1.8 kg/ 3¼–4 lb.
1 lemon, cut in half
3 tablespoons Dijon mustard
1 tablespoon herbes de Provence
5 egg whites
1.8 kg/4 lb. coarse sea salt
cracked black pepper

SERVES 6

INDIAN SPICED LEG OF LAMB COOKED IN A SALT CRUST

This is a simple way to cook lamb – coat it in a thick salt crust and roast it in the oven. The aromas from the spices are intoxicating.

leg of lamb, about 1.3 kg/3 lb., bone in

4 garlic cloves, sliced

SPICE RUB

20 green cardamom pods, bashed

1 teaspoon cumin seeds

1 cinnamon stick, broken into pieces

½ teaspoon whole cloves

½ teaspoon turmeric

½ teaspoon chipotle chilli/chili powder

½ teaspoon Spanish smoked paprika

2 tablespoons olive oil

SALT CRUST

550 g/1¼ lb. coarse sea salt

450 g/3½ cups plain/all-purpose flour, plus extra for dusting

small bunch of curry leaves

RAITA

225 ml/scant 1 cup natural/plain yogurt

2 garlic cloves, finely chopped

1 small cucumber, grated

2 tablespoons mint leaves, torn

sea salt

ground sumac, to sprinkle

SERVES 6–8

Wash the leg of lamb and pat dry. Using a sharp knife, stab the lamb all over and stud with the slices of garlic. Set aside.

Put all the dry ingredients for the spice rub in a saucepan and dry roast over a low heat, stirring continuously, until they are lightly toasted. Pound the toasted spices to a rough mixture using a pestle and mortar. Add the olive oil and stir to a paste. Spread the paste all over the lamb and chill in the refrigerator for at least 2 hours or for up to 24 hours.

When ready to cook the lamb, preheat the oven to 180°C fan/200°C/400°F/Gas 6.

To make the salt crust, mix the salt, flour and curry leaves in a bowl with 250 ml/1 cup water to give a doughy consistency. If the mixture is too dry, add more water, a tablespoon at a time. Roll out on a floured worktop to twice the size of the lamb. Put the lamb leg at one end of the pastry and fold over the remaining dough. Seal, making sure there are no holes for any steam to escape. Put in a lightly oiled roasting tin and bake in the preheated oven for 1 hour.

Once cooked, leave to rest for 10–15 minutes.

To make the raita, mix together the yogurt, garlic, grated cucumber and mint leaves. Season with sea salt and sprinkle with the sumac. Refrigerate until needed.

To serve the lamb, peel off the crust and place on a wooden board to carve. Serve with the raita.

SPICY PORK SATAY WITH ROAST SALTED PEANUT SAUCE

These spicy pork skewers dipped in peanut sauce are heaven on a stick. They are great for weekend get-togethers, when you want to make delicious, easy food with minimum kitchen time. You can also pop these on a barbecue and forgo the hob/stovetop.

450 g/1 lb. pork tenderloin

coriander/cilantro leaves and lime wedges, to garnish

SPICY MARINADE

2 tablespoons rice wine vinegar

2 green chillies/chiles, chopped

1 tablespoon soy sauce

1 large garlic clove, finely chopped

1 tablespoon toasted sesame oil

2 tablespoons fish sauce

2 tablespoons peanut oil

2 tablespoons chopped coriander/cilantro leaves

1 tablespoon grated fresh ginger

ROAST SALTED PEANUT SAUCE

1 tablespoon peanut oil

1 garlic clove, finely chopped

2 red Thai chillies/chiles, finely chopped

4 kaffir lime leaves

1 stalk lemongrass, cut into 4 pieces

1 teaspoon garam masala or curry powder

2 tablespoons dark brown sugar

1 quantity Salty Peanut Butter (see page 26)

250 ml/1 cup coconut milk

30 g/¾ cup unsweetened coconut flakes

finely grated zest and freshly squeezed juice of 1 lime

2 tablespoons fish sauce

18–20 wooden skewers, soaked in cold water for 30 minutes

MAKES 18–20 SKEWERS

Slice the pork into 5 mm/¼ inch thick pieces and put in a bowl Mix together all the spicy marinade ingredients and pour over the pork. Cover and put in the refrigerator for 30 minutes.

To make the roast salted peanut sauce, heat the peanut oil in a saucepan over a medium heat. Sauté the garlic, chillies, kaffir lime leaves, lemongrass and garam masala for 2 minutes. Add the sugar and stir. Now add the salty peanut butter, coconut milk and coconut flakes, along with the lime zest and juice. Cook for 15 minutes. Take off the heat and stir in the fish sauce. Pour the mixture into a bowl and set aside.

Remove the pork from the refrigerator and thread onto the soaked wooden skewers.

Heat a ridged griddle pan over a high heat until nearly smoking. Grill the pork skewers for 3-4 minutes on each side until cooked through, brown and caramelized.

Garnish the pork skewers with coriander leaves and serve with lime wedges and the roast salted peanut sauce.

ROSEMARY AND GARLIC-BRINED ROASTED RACK OF PORK

This slow-roasted rack of pork – smothered in a peach and rosemary glaze that's been enriched with rosé wine – is, quite simply, delicious! As a rack of pork is a lean meat, despite the blanket of fat, overcooking it can make it tough. To avoid this, here the meat is brined for a few hours before cooking. This will ensure a succulent and mouthwatering roast. Recipe pictured on page 70.

pork rack, about 2–2.5 kg/ 5¼–5½ lb., French trimmed, skinned, fat left on

250 g/9 oz. salt

200 g/1 cup white sugar, for brining, plus 1–2 teaspoons extra, to taste

1 whole garlic bulb (about 10–12 cloves)

6 sprigs rosemary

6 dried bay leaves

1 tablespoon olive oil

6 ripe peaches, stoned/pitted and chopped

250 ml/1 cup rosé or white wine

1 white onion, thickly sliced

knob/pat of butter

salt and cracked black pepper

simple green salad and fried potatoes, to serve

SERVES 6–8

Making the brine couldn't be easier. Find a large non-reactive container (plastic, glass or stainless steel) big enough to take the whole rack of pork. Put the salt and 200 g/1 cup of sugar in the container with about 1 litre/quart cold water and stir until fully dissolved. Add half of the rosemary sprigs, about 6 garlic cloves, lightly cracked (you can leave the skin on), and the bay leaves. Submerge the whole rack of pork in the brine. Cover and keep in the fridge for a few hours. (If you can't fit it in your fridge, add ice cubes to the water to keep it chilled, or you can even put it outside if it's a cold day.) You will need to remove the pork from the brine 30 minutes before you plan to cook it, to dry it and bring it to room temperature.

While the pork is in the brine, make the glaze. Crush 2 garlic cloves and add to a small saucepan with the olive oil. Set over a low heat and just warm the garlic through (without letting it colour), then add the leaves stripped from half a rosemary sprig followed by the peaches, wine (reserving a splash to deglaze the roasting pan later) and 1 teaspoon sugar. Season with salt and pepper and simmer for 15 minutes over a low heat, uncovered, until the peaches have broken down but still retain a little texture. Taste, as depending on the sweetness of your peaches and wine, you may want to add a little more sugar.

Remove from the heat, siphon off one-third of the mixture and reserve for the sauce.

Preheat the oven to 200°C fan/220°C/425°F/Gas 7.

Scatter the onion slices, any remaining garlic cloves (lightly cracked with the skin on) and the remaining sprigs of rosemary into a large roasting pan and place the pork on top. Score the fat on the pork with a small sharp knife, without piercing the flesh, and season with salt and pepper. Spoon over two-thirds of the peach glaze.

Roast the pork in the preheated oven for 1½ hours. Remove from the oven, transfer to a tray and loosely cover with aluminium foil. Let rest for 30 minutes (this resting period is important as it ensures the meat finishes cooking internally and is tender).

Set the roasting pan and its contents over a low heat and add the reserved splash of wine. Heat, scraping off any of the burnt bits, and simmer for 5 minutes until the wine has reduced by half. Remove from the heat, add the butter and the remaining peach glaze and whisk it in until emulsified. Pass through a sieve/strainer into a sauce jug/pitcher.

Put the rested pork rack on a large wooden board ready to be carved and serve with the jug of warmed peach glaze on the side for pouring. The perfect accompaniments to this are a simple green salad and crisply fried potatoes.

BEEF TRI-TIP POKE

This Californian poke dish uses tri-tip beef (a cut from the bottom sirloin), but you can substitute topside (preferably the corner cut) or bavette/goose skirt. The salty dry rub gives it a wonderful flavour.

1.5 kg/3¼ lb. beef tri-tip or topside corner cut, or bavette/goose skirt

DRY RUB

1 tablespoon cumin seeds
1 tablespoon coriander seeds
1 teaspoon smoked paprika
1½ tablespoons sea salt

PINTO BEANS

3 rashers/slices smoked streaky/fatty bacon, chopped
150 g/5½ oz. smoked cooked ham, diced
400-g/14-oz. can chopped tomatoes
3 garlic cloves, chopped
2 teaspoons dark soy sauce
2 teaspoons ketjap manis (Indonesian soy sauce)
1 teaspoon chipotle paste
1 teaspoon smoked paprika
400-g/14-oz. can pinto beans (or black beans), drained and rinsed

TO SERVE

250 g/9 oz. kale, cooked and finely chopped
salsa or ketchup

SERVES 6

For the dry rub, heat a dry frying pan/skillet and lightly toast the cumin and coriander seeds. When slightly coloured, grind to a coarse powder using a mortar and pestle. Add the smoked paprika and salt. Rub the mixture all over the meat.

To oven-roast topside or tri-tip, preheat the oven to 200°C fan/220°C/425°F/Gas 7. Place the beef in a roasting pan and roast for 15 minutes to seal the surfaces, then loosely cover with foil and reduce the heat to 160°C fan/180°C/350°F/Gas 4 for 30 minutes, or until the inside is medium-rare. Baste occasionally with pan juices. At the end of the cooking time, remove the foil and turn the heat right up to brown the meat.

To cook bavette/goose skirt in a ridged pan, lightly oil the meat. Heat the pan to very hot, add the meat, leave for 3 minutes, then turn over for 3 minutes. Turn again but at right angles for another 3 minutes, then turn again at right angles for a final 3 minutes. This should give you a rare to medium-rare result. Leave a little longer if undercooked.

For the pinto beans, heat a large frying pan/skillet and add the bacon and diced ham. When browned, add the remaining ingredients apart from the beans. Turn down the heat and simmer for 20 minutes. Add the beans and 500 ml/2 cups water and simmer for another 20 minutes.

To serve, dice the meat into 1-cm/½-inch cubes. Place some kale in bowls, followed by the pinto beans and beef. Top with red salsa or ketchup.

UMAMI STEAK TAGLIATA

This salty rub is a beautiful thing, but with good-quality steak and a drizzle of green extra virgin olive oil, it is ridiculously sublime. This rub recipe makes more than you need for two steaks but you can store the excess in a tightly sealed jar and use on other meats and fish.

Start with the garlic pesto. Using a mortar and pestle, pound together the garlic, rosemary, black peppercorns and a good pinch of salt to a chunky pesto consistency. Add just enough olive oil to form a loose pesto and set aside.

Next make the rub. Start by grinding the dried mushrooms to a powder in the mortar and pestle; you should have about 1 tablespoon once ground. Tip into a bowl with all the other rub ingredients in a bowl and mix together well.

Generously rub each steak all over with about a tablespoon of the rub. Once they are well coated, place the steaks on a plate and drizzle with some of the garlic pesto, keeping the rest aside. If time permits, cover the steaks in clingfilm/plastic wrap and leave them for 20–30 minutes to come to room temperature.

Preheat a frying pan/skillet over a medium-high heat. Once hot, cook the steaks to your liking.

Once cooked, remove the steaks from the pan and leave to rest for a minute or so in a warm place.

To serve, slice diagonally with a sharp knife and serve on warmed plates topped with any pan juices, an extra spoonful of the garlic pesto, and a good drizzle of extra virgin olive oil.

2 steaks (rib-eye, New York strip/sirloin, or filet mignon/fillet)
extra virgin olive oil, to drizzle

GARLIC PESTO

2 large garlic cloves
leaves from 2 sprigs rosemary
5 black peppercorns
sea salt
extra virgin olive oil, as needed

UMAMI RUB
(MAKES 120 G/4 OZ.)

handful of dried mushrooms (shiitake, porcini, or a mix)
2 tablespoons sea salt
1 tablespoon brown sugar
1 tablespoon smoked paprika
1 tablespoon dried oregano
2 teaspoons ground cumin
2 teaspoons garlic powder
1 teaspoon cracked black pepper
½ teaspoon cayenne pepper (or to taste)

SERVES 2

SALT AND PEPPER-CRUSTED STEAKS WITH RED WINE SAUCE

This has to be the ultimate fast-food recipe – you can make it from start to finish in just 5 minutes. The red wine gives a wonderful instant sauce that takes the dish into the luxury league. After you have made this a couple of times, you'll find you won't need measurements – just pour in a dash of brandy, half a glass of red wine and a slosh of cream to finish, and away you go.

1 tablespoon mixed
    peppercorns
½ teaspoon sea salt
1 teaspoon plain/all-purpose
    flour
2 thinly cut rump steaks,
    125–150 g/4–5½ oz. each,
    fat removed
1 tablespoon olive oil
25 g/1½ tablespoons butter
2 tablespoons brandy
75 ml/⅓ cup full-bodied fruity
    red wine
3 tablespoons fresh beef
    or chicken stock
1 teaspoon redcurrant jelly
    or a few drops of balsamic
    vinegar (optional)
2 tablespoons crème fraîche
    or sour cream

SERVES 2

Put the peppercorns and salt in a mortar and pound with a pestle until coarsely ground. Tip into a shallow dish and mix in the flour. Dip each steak into the salt and pepper mixture and press the coating in lightly, turning to coat both sides.

Heat a frying pan/skillet pan over a medium heat and add the oil and the butter. Once the butter has melted, add the steaks to the pan and cook for 1½ minutes. Turn them over and cook for 30 seconds on the other side. Transfer the steaks to two warmed plates to rest.

Pour the brandy into the pan and light it carefully with a long cook's match or taper. When the flames die down, add the wine and cook for a few seconds.

Add the stock and simmer for 1–2 minutes. Sweeten with a little redcurrant jelly or balsamic vinegar, if you like, then stir in the crème fraîche or sour cream.

Pour the sauce over the steaks and serve. It is lovely with a rocket/arugula salad and some crusty bread.

SALADS AND SIDES

PEACH CAPRESE WITH CURRY SALT

Summer, when peaches are in season, is the time to make this salad.
The sweet and juicy peaches play off the slightly salty mozzarella,
and a sprinkle of curry salt spices up the whole dish.

Slice the mozzarella balls into 5-mm/¼-inch thick slices.

Cut the peaches in half and remove the stones/pits. Slice the peach halves into 5-mm/¼-inch thick slices. Tear the basil and mint leaves from their stems, reserving 4 mint sprigs to garnish.

To make the vinaigrette, put all the ingredients in a small bowl and whisk together.

To make the curry salt, mix together the fleur de sel and curry powder in a small bowl.

To assemble the salad, put a slice of mozzarella on each plate, then top with a slice of peach. Add a few basil and mint leaves and continue to layer until you have used up all the slices of mozzarella and peach.

Drizzle the vinaigrette over the salads and finish with a sprinkle of curry salt. Garnish each plate with a sprig of mint and serve.

2 x 225-g/8-oz. fresh buffalo
   mozzarella balls
2 large yellow peaches
small bunch mint
small bunch basil

VINAIGRETTE

60 ml/¼ cup Champagne
   vinegar
125 ml/½ cup extra virgin
   olive oil
½ teaspoon honey

CURRY SALT

2 tablespoons fleur de sel
2 teaspoons Madras curry
   powder

SERVES 4

WATERMELON AND RICOTTA SALATA SALAD WITH OLIVE SALT

This is a delightfully pretty and refreshing salad in which the olive salt brings out the sweetness of the watermelon. Ricotta salata, a lightly salted cheese made from sheep's milk, originates from the island of Sicily. If you can't find a mini watermelon, buy the smallest available and cut it in half. You can use feta cheese if ricotta salata isn't available.

1 mini seedless watermelon
170 g/6 oz. ricotta salata cheese
2 tablespoons fresh oregano leaves
olive oil, to drizzle
cracked black pepper

OLIVE SALT

10 stoned/pitted black olives
2½ tablespoons sea salt

SERVES 2

Peel the watermelon and cut it into bite-sized chunks. Put in a serving bowl, crumble the ricotta salata over the watermelon and sprinkle with the oregano.

To make the olive salt, chop the olives roughly. Grind them with the salt using a pestle and mortar until the olives are mashed.

Drizzle some olive oil over the salad and season with black pepper. Sprinkle with a generous amount of the olive salt. Put the remainder of the salt in a bowl to use on other dishes.

SALT-BAKED BEETROOT WITH WILD GARLIC

Here, salt-baking the beetroot both intensifies the flavour and seasons it, while the wild garlic leaves and flowers provide a subtle garlicky backdrop. If you have wild garlic flowers you can add these to the salad as a final garnish.

Preheat the oven to 160°C fan/180°C/360°F/Gas 4.

First make the salt crust by whisking the egg white, then folding in the salt and sugar. You should have a wet cement-type consistency; add more salt if needed.

Put a little of the salt mixture in the centre of the parchment on the prepared roasting pan to make a bed for the beetroots to sit on. Group the beetroots together on top of this, add the thyme sprigs and spoon the remaining salt mixture over the top, ensuring the beetroots are fully covered. Bake in the oven for 1½–2 hours, depending on the size of the beetroots.

Once done, leave to cool for 10 minutes before breaking open the salt crust. Remove the beetroots and, while they are still warm (but cool enough to handle), peel the skins off. If they go cold, the skin is harder to peel.

Slice the beetroots into discs about 5 mm/¼ inch thick. (A good life hack is to rub olive oil on your hands before touching the beetroot and it stops it staining your fingers!)

Slice the garlic as thinly as you can and scatter it over the beetroot. Season with black pepper and drizzle with olive oil and vinegar. Roughly slice the wild garlic leaves, leaving a few whole just for show, and gently fold all the ingredients together. Serve at room temperature.

1 egg white
350 g/12 oz. coarse rock salt
150 g/¾ cup sugar
4–5 small beetroots/beets (about 350 g/12 oz.)
a few sprigs thyme
1 small garlic clove
12 wild garlic/ramps leaves
cracked black pepper
olive oil, to drizzle
red wine vinegar, to drizzle

roasting pan or deep-sided baking sheet, lined with baking parchment

SERVES 6

TRINI SALTFISH BULJOL

This is a great introduction to Caribbean food and the many varied ways of using salt cod (saltfish to West Indians and bacalao to Spaniards). It might look like an unpromising ingredient but you can't help but become a fan when it delivers flavours like these.

225 g/8 oz. salt cod
200 ml/generous ¾ cup milk
1 fresh bay leaf
1 slice of lemon
25 g/2 tablespoons butter
5–6 mixed peppercorns
1 teaspoon Dijon mustard
1 large onion, very finely chopped
1 large tomato, diced
1 ripe pointed red sweet (bell) pepper, deseeded and diced, or ordinary red sweet (bell) pepper
1 Trinidad Congo chilli/chile, deseeded and finely chopped*
1 Hungarian Hot Wax chilli/chile, deseeded and finely chopped
½ teaspoon cracked black pepper
3 tablespoons olive oil
a few Cos/Romaine lettuce leaves
2 hard-boiled/hard-cooked eggs, sliced
1 avocado, peeled, stoned/pitted and sliced

SERVES 2–4

You will need to start preparing the salad the day before you serve it. Put the salt cod in a bowl, cover with cold water and let soak for 24 hours in the fridge, changing the water frequently.

The next day, drain the soaked cod and pat dry with kitchen paper/paper towels. Put the cod in a large frying pan/skillet and add the milk, bay leaf, lemon, butter and peppercorns. Cover with a lid and poach gently for 20 minutes, or until the fish is soft. Remove from the poaching liquor (reserving the liquor) and let cool.

Flake the fish into a bowl, removing the bones.

Return the pan of poaching liquor to a medium heat and cook, stirring regularly to prevent a skin forming. Once the liquid has reduced by half, remove the bay leaf, lemon and peppercorns and discard. Remove from the heat and stir in the mustard. Let cool for a while, until thickened.

To the flaked fish, add the onion, tomato, sweet pepper, chillies, black pepper and olive oil and mix well. Serve on the lettuce leaves and garnish with the eggs and avocado. Serve with the thickened milk/mustard combination in a small bowl.

* Trinidad Congo chillies are members of the Habanero family of chillies. They are renowned for their pungency and wonderful fruity flavour and aroma. If you can't get hold of these, any Habanero/Scotch Bonnet variety of chilli will work perfectly in this recipe. Hungarian Hot Wax chillies are mild peppers that add a delicious crunch and a modest kick to any salad. If these are not available, substitute with half a yellow sweet (bell) pepper.

HOME-CURED DUCK WITH ROCKET AND ORANGE VINAIGRETTE

It takes a good few days to cure and then needs another few days to rest, but this is a great way of preserving a duck breast to use over a couple of weeks. Increase the curing time for a larger duck breast.

Trim the duck breast of any trailing bits of fat, and if it has a very thick layer of fat on top, lightly trim this as well. Use a sharp knife to score the skin in diagonal line without piercing the flesh.

To make the curing salt mixture, simply mix together the salt, sugar, black pepper and ground bay leaf in a small bowl.

Choose a non-reactive dish (ceramic or glass is best) into which the duck breast will fit snugly. Scatter one-third of the curing salt mixture in the bottom (or enough to create a complete layer), then lay the duck flesh-side down and cover with the remaining mixture. Add more salt if any of the duck is exposed; you need it to be fully encased. Cover the top of the dish with clingfilm/plastic wrap and refrigerate for 3 days.

After 3 days the duck will have shrunk a little and be much firmer. Rinse off the salt, pat it with kitchen paper/paper towels until fully dry and then loosely wrap it in baking parchment (you don't want it to be airtight, it needs a little air to allow the moisture to escape). Return it to the fridge for a further 5 days before serving.

When you are ready to serve, make the dressing by whisking together the orange juice, olive oil and vinegar until emulsified and season with a pinch each of salt and pepper. Slice the duck very thinly, starting at the thinner end and cutting at an angle. Arrange the slices on a plate with a little rocket, dressed with the orange vinaigrette and a sprinkle of orange zest.

You can store any leftover duck, unsliced, in the fridge in an airtight container so that it doesn't dry out, for up to 2 weeks.

250-g/9-oz. duck breast
2 tablespoons freshly squeezed orange juice, plus a little finely grated orange zest to garnish
4 tablespoons extra virgin olive oil
1 tablespoon cider vinegar
salt and cracked black pepper
a few handfuls of rocket/arugula

CURING SALT MIXTURE

400 g/14 oz. coarse sea salt
50 g/¼ cup demerara/turbinado sugar
1 tablespoon cracked black pepper
1 dried bay leaf, ground to a powder with a pestle and mortar

MAKES 12 SERVINGS

STEAK FRIES WITH SEASONED SALT

Coarse-cut and with their skins on, these are rough, ready and tasty, too. Something about their size means they marry well with powerful flavours, so it's a good idea to use strong spices or dips. The seasoning mix here is based on a popular American seasoning salt and is an excellent all-rounder.

3 large floury potatoes, all roughly the same size

vegetable or sunflower oil, for deep-frying

SEASONED SALT

2 tablespoons fine salt

1 teaspoon caster/granulated sugar

½ teaspoon celery salt

½ teaspoon paprika

¼ teaspoon ground turmeric

¼ teaspoon onion granules

¼ teaspoon garlic granules

pinch of cayenne pepper

SERVES 4 AS A SIDE

In a small bowl, combine the seasoning ingredients and mix well to blend. Set aside.

Scrub the potatoes well and dry. Do not peel. Cut the potatoes into long thin pieces, not as big as a wedge, but not as small as a French fry.

Put the potatoes into a bowl of iced water for at least 5 minutes, to remove excess starch and prevent sticking when frying.

Fill a large saucepan one-third full with the oil or, if using a deep-fryer, follow the manufacturer's instructions. Heat the oil to 190°C (375°F). To test if the oil is hot enough, drop a cube of bread in the oil; it should turn golden brown in 20 seconds.

Drain the potatoes and dry very well. Working in batches, fry a handful of potatoes at a time. Place the potatoes in a frying basket and lower into the hot oil carefully. Fry for 4 minutes. Remove and drain on kitchen paper/paper towels. Repeat until all of the potatoes have been fried.

Just before serving, skim any debris off the top of the cooking oil and reheat to the same temperature.

Fry as before, working in batches, but only cook until crisp and golden, about 2 minutes. Remove and drain on paper towels. Repeat until all of the potatoes have been fried.

Serve with the seasoned salt on the side.

ROASTED CHERRY TOMATOES WITH OLIVES AND FLEUR DE SEL

This is the perfect dish to serve with fish. It's delicious and simple, with the added bonus of the wonderful aroma of rosemary while cooking. Use tiny black Niçoise olives – their intense flavour goes very well with the sweet tomatoes. Recipe pictured on page 96.

1 sprig rosemary
450 g/1 lb. cherry tomatoes
90 g/scant 1 cup stoned/
    pitted Niçoise olives
fleur de sel and cracked
    black pepper

SERVES 4

Preheat the oven to 170°C fan/190°C/375°F/Gas 5.

Run your fingers down the rosemary sprig, tearing the leaves off as you go. It will yield about 2 tablespoons of leaves.

In a bowl, toss together the rosemary, tomatoes and olives. Season with cracked black pepper.

Pour the tomato mixture in a non-stick baking sheet or tin. Roast in the preheated oven for 10 minutes until the tomatoes have some colour and have softened. Remove from the oven and shake the tray. Set aside to cool for a few minutes.

Put the tomatoes and olives in a bowl, sprinkle with the fleur de sel and serve.

BARBECUE CORN ON THE COB WITH SMOKED SALT PIMENTO BUTTER

Cook corn on the cob on the barbecue, tear off the outer husks and slather in smoked pimento butter to enjoy the deep, smoky flavours. Keep leftover butter in the refrigerator for up to 1 week; it will go well with any grilled meat. Recipe pictured on page 96.

Put the butter in a food processor with the paprika and smoked sea salt. Mix until the butter is smooth. Cover and refrigerate until ready to use.

Preheat a barbecue.

Put the corn on the cob, with the husks still on, on the hot barbecue. Cook for 3 minutes, turn over and cook for another 3 minutes. You want the corn to have a crunch when you bite into it.

When the corn is ready, remove from the heat and tear back the outer husk. You can use the husk as a handle. Spread the smoked salt pimento butter over the corn and eat immediately.

225 g/2 sticks unsalted butter, at room temperature

2 teaspoons sweet smoked paprika

1 teaspoon smoked sea salt

6 corn on the cob, husks still on

SERVES 6

GRILLED SUMMER COURGETTE WITH BASIL SALT

Grilling the courgettes and their flowers on hot coals, then sprinkling with basil salt is simple and perfect for any occasion.

65 g/2 oz. coarse sea salt

12 large basil leaves

16 green and golden courgettes/zucchini

120 ml/½ cup avocado oil

60 ml/¼ cup Champagne vinegar

10 courgette/zucchini flowers, stamens removed

sea salt and cracked black pepper

oil, for brushing

1 sterilized glass jar with a lid*

SERVES 6

Preheat the oven to 100°C fan/120°C/250°F/Gas ½.

Pulse together the salt and basil in a food processor, then spread the mixture out on a baking sheet. Bake in the preheated oven for 30 minutes until dry. Pour into a sterilized glass jar with a tight-fitting lid and set aside. (Any unused basil salt will keep for 2 weeks stored this way.)

Slice the courgettes in half lengthways (or quarter them if they are large) and arrange on a baking sheet. Whisk together the oil and vinegar and season with salt and pepper. Pour this over the courgettes and toss to make sure they are well covered.

Heat the barbecue to medium-high. Brush the grate with oil.

Grill the courgettes for 3-4 minutes on each side until they are slightly charred and golden brown, then plate. Place the courgette flowers on the grill and cook for about a minute on each side, then add to the courgettes.

Sprinkle with the basil salt and cracked black pepper and serve.

*To sterilize, wash the jar in hot soapy water and rinse. Place in a preheated oven at 160°C fan/180°C/350°F/Gas 4 for 10 minutes.

ROASTED CARROTS AND LEGUMES WITH SALT AND PINK PEPPERCORNS

This is a warming, earthy side dish, which works well as part of a winter menu, but it could also be served at summer barbecues – so it really is enjoyable at any time of the year. The crispy, popped legumes will capture the hearts of even the least adventurous, potentially young, among us. If you're cooking for children, you could grind the pink peppercorns a little to avoid them getting a whole one mid-bite.

Preheat the oven to 200°C fan/220°C/425°F/Gas 7.

Halve the carrots lengthways (if you're using baby, or just slim carrots, leave whole). Add the prepped carrots, chickpeas, haricot beans, garlic cloves, olive oil, salt and peppercorns to a large baking sheet and toss well to coat. Roast on the top shelf of the preheated oven for 1 hour, turning halfway through cooking.

Once ready, add the chopped parsley, then fold through the roasted carrots and legumes. Serve immediately.

6 carrots (or 12 baby carrots)

400-g/14-oz. can chickpeas/ garbanzo beans, drained and rinsed

400-g/14-oz. can haricot/ navy beans, drained and rinsed

8 garlic cloves (skin-on)

3 tablespoons olive oil

2 teaspoons sea salt

2 teaspoons pink peppercorns

10 g/⅓ oz. parsley, roughly chopped

SERVES 4–6

TALEGGIO AND GRAPE FOCACCIA WITH ROSEMARY AND SEA SALT

This gorgeously gooey bread with its salty top makes a great accompaniment for a selection of antipasti.

250 g/1¾ cups strong white bread flour, plus extra for dusting

250 g/generous 1¾ cups 00 flour

1 teaspoon fast-action dried yeast

1 teaspoon caster/superfine sugar

2 teaspoons fine sea salt

300 ml/1¼ cups hand-hot water

2–3 tablespoons olive oil

fine semolina, for dusting (optional)

30 g/1 oz. Parmesan cheese, grated

175 g/6 oz. Taleggio, cut into thin slices

75 g/2½ oz. Gorgonzola, cut into thin slices

150g/5½ oz. red seedless grapes

2 sprigs rosemary

coarse sea salt and cracked black pepper

32 x 18-cm/13 x 7-inch baking tin, lightly greased

MAKES 1

Put the two flours into a large bowl. Add the yeast, sugar and salt, mix together well, then hollow out a hole in the centre. Pour in the water and 1 tablespoon olive oil, then bring the mixture together, first with a wooden spoon and then with your hands, adding a little extra water if needed. Tip the dough out onto a lightly floured surface and knead for about 5–6 minutes until it is smooth and springs back when you press it with a finger.

Put the dough in a lightly oiled bowl, cover and leave to rise for about 45 minutes, or until doubled in size. Knock back the dough, give it a couple of swift turns, then cut in two pieces, one slightly bigger than the other. Dust the baking tin with semolina, if you have some. Stretch and press the larger of the two pieces into the tin, so that it covers the base and comes up the sides.

Sprinkle over the Parmesan, then add the sliced Taleggio and Gorgonzola, and scatter with the grapes. Season well with black pepper. Roll out and stretch the other piece of bread dough to fit over the filling, bringing up the dough underneath and pressing to seal round the sides. Cover with clingfilm/plastic wrap or a towel and leave for another 30 minutes or so to rise.

About 15 minutes before you think the dough will be ready, turn the oven to 200°C fan/220°C/425°F/Gas 7. Using the tips of your fingers, make deep indentations in the dough, taking care not to deflate the bread, and tuck the rosemary into the holes. Brush the surface lightly with olive oil and season with coarse sea salt.

Bake for 10 minutes, then turn the heat down to 180°C fan/200°C/400°F/Gas 6 and cook for another 15 minutes until well risen. Drizzle with a little more olive oil, leave to cool for 5–10 minutes then cut into squares or strips.

SWEET THINGS

CHOCOLATE SEA SALT COOKIES

You may think this combination sounds a little odd, but it really is a divine cookie. One bite and you will experience the explosion of tastes between the dark rich sweetness of the chocolate and the fleur de sel salt. Use only the best fleur de sel from Guérande in France for the best flavour.

140 g/generous 1 cup plain/all-purpose flour

40 g/generous ⅓ cup cocoa powder

½ teaspoon baking powder

½ teaspoon bicarbonate of soda/baking soda

120 g/4 oz. dark/bittersweet chocolate (70% cocoa solids), roughly chopped

170 g/1½ sticks unsalted butter, at room temperature

85 g/7 tablespoons dark brown sugar

40 g/3¼ tablespoons caster/granulated sugar

1 egg

1 teaspoon pure vanilla extract

1 teaspoon rum

fleur de sel, to sprinkle

2 baking sheets, lined with baking parchment

MAKES 24

Preheat the oven to 160°C fan/180°C/350°F/Gas 4.

Sift together the flour, cocoa powder, baking powder and bicarbonate of soda and set aside.

Melt 40 g/1½ oz. of the chocolate, either in a bowl set over a saucepan of simmering water or in a microwave.

Cream together the butter and sugars in a food processor on high speed until light and fluffy, scraping down the sides of the bowl if necessary. Add the egg, vanilla extract, rum and melted chocolate. Continue to beat for 2 minutes. Reduce the speed to slow and add the flour mixture. When that is well mixed, stir in the remaining chopped chocolate.

Put the mixture in the refrigerator for 5 minutes to harden slightly. Scoop tablespoons of the mixture onto the lined baking sheets, 5 cm/2 inches apart (a small ice cream scoop is good for this). Flatten slightly with the back of the scoop. Sprinkle a little fleur de sel on top of each cookie and bake in the preheated oven for 10 minutes.

Leave to cool slightly on the baking sheets before transferring to a wire rack to cool completely.

MEXICAN CHOCOLATE CHILLI-SALTED TRUFFLES

A spicy taste from Mexico, these salty chilli chocolate truffles, rolled in Mexican Ibarra chocolate and Himalayan pink rock salt, are divine! You won't be able to stop eating them. Mexican Ibarra chocolate discs are made with chocolate mixed with cocoa beans and cinnamon. Buy them at Latin food markets.

Put the chopped chocolate, cream and butter in a heatproof bowl. Place the bowl over a pan of simmering water, making sure the water does not touch the bottom of the bowl. Once the chocolate has started to melt, stir gently until the mixture is smooth and creamy.

Stir in the chilli oil and pour the mixture into a shallow bowl. Refrigerate until firm.

To make the dusting powder, process the Ibarra chocolate to a powder in a food processor. Pour it into a bowl and mix in the Himalayan salt.

When the chocolate mixture has set, scoop out the truffles with the melon baller and roll into balls. Toss in the dusting powder and serve.

*If you can't find Ibarra chocolate, you can make a similar dusting powder by blitzing the following ingredients in a food processor: 55 g/¼ cup caster/granulated sugar, 20 g/scant ¼ cup cocoa powder, 1 teaspoon ground cinnamon and 1 tablespoon Himalayan pink rock salt.

220 g/8 oz. dark/bittersweet chocolate (70% cocoa solids), roughly chopped
60 ml/¼ cup single/light cream
1 tablespoon unsalted butter
½ teaspoon confectioner's chilli/chili oil, or to taste

SALTED COCOA DUSTING POWDER*

90 g/3 oz. Ibarra chocolate discs, roughly chopped
1 tablespoon Himalayan pink rock salt

melon baller

MAKES 40

SALTED CARAMEL BROWNIES

Brownies are best when ever-so-slightly undercooked and fudgy. This salted caramel version has a sprinkle of cocoa nibs for a bitter crunch.

150 g/1 stick plus
    2 tablespoons unsalted
    butter
200 g/7 oz. dark/bittersweet
    (70%) chocolate, chopped
4 eggs, beaten
200 g/1 cup light brown sugar
100 g/½ cup caster/
    granulated sugar
pinch of salt
1 teaspoon pure vanilla paste
    or extract
80 g/⅔ cup plain/all-purpose
    flour, sifted
1 tablespoon cocoa nibs
    (optional)
cocoa powder, to dust
    (optional)

SALTED CARAMEL

100 g/½ cup caster/superfine
    sugar
3 tablespoons golden/light
    corn syrup
4 tablespoons double/heavy
    cream
30 g/2 tablespoons unsalted
    butter
pinch of fleur de sel or flaky
    sea salt

23 x 23-cm/9 x 9-in. brownie pan,
    lined with baking parchment

MAKES 40–50

Preheat the oven to 150°C fan/170°C/325°F/Gas 3.

For the salted caramel, put the sugar and syrup in a small saucepan over a medium heat. Swirl the pan but do not stir. When the sugar is a copper colour, take off the heat and slowly whisk in the cream. Add the butter and salt, and gently whisk. Set aside.

Melt the butter and chocolate in a heatproof bowl set over a saucepan of gently simmering water, taking care that the water is not in contact with the bowl. Transfer to a large bowl. Add the eggs, along with the sugars, salt and vanilla. Fold in the flour.

Pour into the prepared pan and smooth the top. Drizzle the caramel onto the surface and use a skewer to swirl it around. Sprinkle over the nibs, if using, and bake for 20–25 minutes; it should still have a slight wobble in the centre.

Allow to cool in the pan and then cut into squares. You could also cut into smaller squares and dust in cocoa powder to make a bite-sized brownie truffle, if liked.

CHOCOLATE AND SALTED CARAMEL PEANUT SLICE

The salted peanuts help to cut through the intense sweetness of the caramel and add a lovely crunch.

Preheat the oven to 160°C fan/180°C/350°F/Gas 4.

Place the flour, coconut and caster sugar in a large mixing bowl. Pour the melted butter over the dry ingredients, mix together and press firmly into the base of the prepared baking pan. Bake in the preheated oven for about 15 minutes, or until light golden in colour. Remove from the oven and set aside to cool.

To make the caramel layer, place the unopened can of condensed milk on a folded kitchen towel in a deep saucepan or pot to stop it rattling while it boils. Cover completely with warm water and bring to the boil over a medium–high heat. Reduce the heat to low and simmer for 4 hours.

Remove from the water and leave the can to cool before opening it – it will have magically transformed into caramel.

In a separate saucepan set over a medium heat, melt the butter with the light brown sugar, until the sugar has completely dissolved. Add the cooked condensed milk, reduce the heat and simmer for 10 minutes until the mixture has thickened slightly.

Pour the hot caramel mixture over the baked base and sprinkle the salted peanuts evenly across the top.

To make the topping, melt the chocolate and cream together in a heatproof bowl set over a pan of simmering water, making sure the base of the bowl doesn't touch the water below. Pour evenly over the caramel layer and chill in the fridge to set.

Once set, remove from the fridge and sprinkle with coarse sea salt. Cut into even squares and serve stacked high on a plate.

120 g/1 cup self-raising/self-rising flour

70 g/1 scant cup shredded/desiccated coconut

75 g/⅓ cup caster/granulated sugar

110 g/7 tablespoons unsalted butter, melted

SALTED CARAMEL PEANUTS

400-g/14-oz. can sweetened condensed milk

120 g/1 stick unsalted butter

120 g/½ cup soft light brown sugar

100 g/⅔ cup roasted salted peanuts, roughly chopped

TOPPING

150 g/1¼ cups chopped dark/bittersweet chocolate

100 ml/scant ½ cup double/heavy cream

coarse sea salt, to decorate (optional)

20 x 30-cm/8 x 12-in baking pan, greased and lined with baking parchment

MAKES 20

RICE PUDDING WITH SALTED CARAMEL SAUCE

Traditionally, rice pudding contains raisins, and in this pimped up version, the sweetness of the raisins is enhanced with salted caramel and pistachios, adding crunch and texture.

1 litre/quart whole/full-fat milk

140 g/⅔ cup short grain white rice

pinch of salt

2 eggs

50 g/¼ cup dark muscovado sugar

1 teaspoon pure vanilla extract

¼ teaspoon ground cinnamon

handful of raisins, sultanas/golden raisins and crushed pistachios, to garnish (optional)

SALTED CARAMEL SAUCE

200 g/1 cup caster/granulated sugar

175 ml/¾ cup double/heavy cream

1 teaspoon fleur de sel

SERVES 4

Put the milk, rice and pinch of salt in a heavy-bottomed saucepan and set over a high heat. Bring to the boil, then reduce the heat to low and simmer for 20–25 minutes until the rice is tender. Stir frequently with a wooden spoon to prevent the rice from sticking to the bottom of the pan.

In a small mixing bowl, whisk together the eggs and brown sugar until well mixed. Add 125 ml/½ cup of the hot rice mixture to the egg mixture, a tablespoon at a time, vigorously whisking to incorporate it.

Return the egg mixture to the saucepan of rice and milk and cook, over a low heat, for 5–10 minutes, stirring continuously until thickened. Be careful not to let the mixture come to the boil at this point or it will curdle. Remove from the heat and stir in the vanilla extract and cinnamon. Spoon the pudding into a serving dish and chill in the refrigerator until ready to serve.

For the salted caramel sauce, combine the sugar and 60 ml/¼ cup water in a small saucepan. Heat the mixture over a low heat, stirring occasionally until the sugar is completely dissolved. Increase the heat to medium and cook without stirring until the syrup turns a rich caramel colour. Remove the pan from the heat and add another 60 ml/¼ cup water and the cream and salt. It will be very hot and may splatter so take care. Transfer to a small jug/pitcher and set aside to cool completely.

When ready to serve, take the rice pudding out of the refrigerator. Scatter over the raisins, sultanas and pistachios (if using). Serve with the salted caramel sauce on the side so more or less can be added to taste, as it is very rich and sweet.

SALTED CARAMEL ICE CREAM

The flavour of salted caramel seems to have come from nowhere to be one of the most celebrated treats from popcorn to fine chocolate. This recipe won't disappoint die-hard fans and will definitely seduce the uninitiated! Serve with a warm brownie or just as it comes.

To make the salted caramel, combine 120 ml/½ cup water and the 400 g/2 cups sugar in a small heavy-bottomed saucepan. Heat the mixture over a low heat, stirring occasionally until the sugar is completely dissolved. Raise the heat to medium and cook without stirring until the syrup turns a rich caramel colour. Stir the vanilla extract and fleur de sel into the caramel and set aside until needed.

Prepare an ice water bath.

Heat the cream in a large saucepan. Once simmering, spoon a little of the cream into the caramel. Return all of the caramel-cream mixture to the pan, add the milk and bring to the boil.

Meanwhile, whisk the egg yolks and the 2 tablespoons sugar together in a large bowl. Once the milk scalds, take it off the heat and add some of the caramel-milk into the eggs, about 60 ml/¼ cup at a time so that you don't cook the eggs. Add the egg and milk mixture to the pan, return to the hob/stove and cook until a sugar thermometer reads 76°C (170°F) or until the mixture coats the back of a spoon.

Strain the custard through a sieve/strainer into a clean bowl and place in the prepared ice bath, stirring occasionally to cool. Cover the mixture and refrigerate for several hours, until it is cold.

Transfer the mixture into an ice-cream maker and churn according to the manufacturer's instructions. Serve immediately for soft-serve or freeze and use within a few days.

400 g/2 cups caster/granulated sugar, plus 2 tablespoons

1 tablespoon pure vanilla extract

2 ½ teaspoons fleur de sel

420 ml/1¾ cups double/heavy cream

1 litre/quart whole/full-fat milk

9 very fresh egg yolks (UK medium/US large)

sugar/candy thermometer
ice-cream maker

MAKES 1 LITRE/QUART

DRINKS

ZESTY MOJITO

This fresh-tasting mojito can either be served simply in jugs/pitchers, or but dust the rim of each glass with a pretty coating of lime salt. Recipe pictured on page 132.

First make a simple syrup. Put the sugar and 250ml/1 cup water in a pan over a medium heat. Simmer until the sugar has dissolved, then set aside to cool completely.

Mix the lime zest and sea salt, spread out on a small plate and set aside.

Muddle the mint and rum in a large jug/pitcher by mashing the mint against the side of the jug with the back of a wooden spoon. Leave for 30 minutes to let the flavours mingle.

Add the cooled syrup, lime juice and soda water to the rum in the jug and stir. Add enough crushed ice to fill the jug. Garnish with mint sprigs.

Wet the rim of a tall glass with a squeezed lime, then dip the glass in the salt mixture and turn once. Do the same with the rest of the glasses then fill up with Mojito.

225 g/1 cup plus 2 tablespoons caster/superfine sugar
finely grated zest of 1 lime
4 tablespoons sea salt flakes
1 large bunch fresh mint, plus extra to garnish
500 ml/2 cups white rum
750 ml/3 cups freshly squeezed lime juice, about 12 limes (reserve the squeezed fruits for the rims)
500 ml/2 cups soda water
crushed ice

SERVES 6

FROZEN PEACH MARGARITA

Peach margarita is best made in season when peaches are ripe and juicy, but you can also use frozen peaches. The chilli salt adds a taste of Mexico. Recipe pictured on page 132.

¼ teaspoon chipotle chilli/chili powder

1 tablespoon Murray River salt flakes

60 ml/¼ cup tequila

30 ml/2 tablespoons peach schnapps

1 large fresh peach, stoned/pitted and quartered, or 225 g/8 oz. frozen peaches

450 g/1 lb. crushed ice

finely grated zest and freshly squeezed juice of 1 lime (reserve the squeezed fruit for the rims)

MAKES 1 LARGE SERVING

Mix together the chilli powder and pink salt flakes. Wet the rim of a glass with the squeezed lime and dip into the pink chilli salt. Set aside.

Put the remaining ingredients in a blender and blend until smooth. Serve in the salted glass.

SALTY LIME SODA

This thirst-quenching drink combining the flavoursome tastes of salt and lime is the ideal sipper for a hot summer's day.

4 teaspoons sea salt
grated zest and freshly
  squeezed juice of 4 limes
400-ml/14-oz. bottle of soda
  water
ice
lime slices, to serve

SERVES 2

Mix together the salt, lime zest and juice and soda water in a jug/pitcher.

Pour into long tall glasses, and serve with ice and lime.

SALTY CHIHUAHUA

This is a tequila variation on the Salty Dog. It's a simple combination that can cut through the fog of any hangover. Try adding a dash of hibiscus cordial for a sweetened variation.

50 ml/2 oz. tequila
200 ml/scant 1 cup grapefruit juice
ice
lime wedge, to garnish
sea salt, for the glass

SERVES 1

Wipe the lime wedge for the garnish around the rim of a highball glass and dip the glass into the sea salt. Fill the glass with ice.

Pour in the tequila and top with the grapefruit juice. Garnish with a lime wedge and serve.

BLACK OLIVE MARTINI

Dry-cured black olives make for a very hip martini. These olives are picked ripe from the tree, washed and dried in the sun, then salted and packed in jars. Skewer them on a rosemary sprig for extra flavour and wow factor.

3 cured stoned/pitted black olives
1 sprig rosemary
1 teaspoon dry vermouth, such as Noilly Prat
ice
60 ml/¼ cup gin

SERVES 1

Skewer the olives on the rosemary sprig.

Pour the vermouth into a chilled glass, swirl and pour out.

Fill a cocktail shaker with ice and pour in the gin. Shake and strain the gin into the glass.

Garnish with the olive skewer and serve immediately.

TRES COMPADRES

The combination of lime, orange and grapefruit juice provide the three citrus compadres. Cointreau and Chambord are then added to the mix to sweeten, and lo and behold, a great cocktail is born. Try serving this long (by adding more fruit juice) for an extra-refreshing cooler with a salted glass rim to elevate.

Wipe the lime wedge for the garnish around the rim of a margarita glass and dip the glass into the sea salt.

Add all the ingredients to a shaker filled with ice. Shake sharply and strain into the salt-rimmed margarita glass. Garnish with a lime wedge.

50 ml/2 oz. Sauza Commemorativo tequila
20 ml/¾ oz. Cointreau
20 ml/¾ oz. Chambord
25 ml/1 oz. freshly squeezed lime juice
20 ml/¾ oz. freshly squeezed orange juice
20 ml/¾ oz. grapefruit juice
ice
lime wedge, to garnish
sea salt, for the glass

SERVES 1

BLOODY MARY WITH CELERY SALT

Bloody Mary, a classic brunch drink, just gets better with a rim of celery salt. When making the celery salt, the leaves are dried in the oven on a wire rack so that warm air can circulate around the leaves.

small bunch celery, with
  leaves
1 tablespoon Jurassic salt
ice
1.25 litres/5 cups chilled
  tomato or vegetable juice
250 ml/1 cup chilled citron
  vodka
3 teaspoons Worcestershire
  sauce
2 teaspoons hot sauce or
  Tabasco sauce
1 tablespoon balsamic vinegar
finely grated zest and freshly
  squeezed juice of 1 lemon
  (reserve the squeezed fruits
  for the rims)
cracked green peppercorns

SERVES 4

Preheat the oven to its lowest setting. Pick the leaves from the celery, place on a wire rack and put in the oven for 10–15 minutes until they are dried. Remove from the oven and leave to cool.

When ready to serve, put the dried celery leaves and Jurassic salt in a mini food processor or a salt grinder, grind and empty onto a small plate. Wet the rims of four glasses with the reserved lemon shells and dip them in the celery salt.

Fill a tall jug with ice and pour in the tomato juice, vodka, Worcestershire sauce, hot sauce, balsamic vinegar and lemon zest and juice. Season liberally with cracked green peppercorns and a little of the celery salt and stir.

Pour into the salt-rimmed glasses. Garnish each with a celery stick and serve.

CLASSIC MARGARITA

A margarita is perhaps the cocktail most associated with a salted glass rim. The first taste of salt before the fresh lime and tequila hit, elevates this drink to another level.

Wipe the lime wedge around the rim of a margarita glass and dip the glass into the sea salt.

Shake all the ingredients sharply with cracked ice, then strain into the salt-rimmed margarita glass.

50 ml/2 oz. gold tequila
25 ml/1 oz. triple sec or Cointreau
25 ml/1 oz. freshly squeezed lime juice
cracked ice
lime wedge, for the glass
sea salt, for the glass

SERVES 1

INDEX

CREDITS

RECIPE CREDITS

All recipes are by Valerie Aikman-Smith, except for the following:

GHILLIE BASAN
Preserved Lemons

FIONA BECKETT
Pepper-crusted Steaks
Rosemary Focaccia

MEGAN DAVIES
Roasted Carrots and Legumes with Salt and Pink Peppercorns
Smoked Salt, Thyme and Brown Butter

URSULA FERRIGNO
Salty Lime Soda

MATT FOLLAS
Salt Cod Brandade

CAROL HILKER
Rice Pudding with Salted Caramel Sauce
Salted Caramel Ice Cream
Trini Saltfish Bujol

THEO A. MICHAELS
Home-cured Anchovies
Home-cured Duck with Rocket and Orange Vinaigrette
Preserved aubergines in Oil
Rosemary and Garlic-brined Roasted Rack of Pork
Salt-baked Beetroot with Wild Garlic

HANNAH MILES
Black Truffle Popcorn

LOUISE PICKFORD
Home-salted Cod with Chorizo and Potatoes

JAMES PORTER
Beef Tri-tip Poke

BEN REED
Classic Margarita
Salty Chihuahua
Tres Compadres

SHELAGH RYAN
Chocolate and salted caramel peanut slice

LAURA SANTINI
Umami Steak Tagliata

FIONA SMITH
Sweet and Sour Pickled Onions

MILLI TAYLOR
Salted caramel brownies

LAURA WASHBURN HUTTON
Matchstick Fries with Sichuan Pepper Salt
Steak Fries with Seasoned Salt

PHOTOGRAPHY CREDITS

All photography is by Jonathon Gregson, except for the following:

ADOBE: AlenKadr
Pages 3, 11, 33, 51, 71, 97, 119, 133.

PETER CASSIDY
Pages 17, 21, 129, 130.

HELEN CATHCART
Pages 118 and 125.

TARA FISHER
Page 39.

RICHARD JUNG
Page 117.

MOWIE KAY
Pages 1, 2, 54, 70, 91, 95, 102, 106.

ERIN KUNKEL
Pages 53, 113.

WILLIAM LINGWOOD
Pages 137, 139, 141.

STEVE PAINTER
Pages 49, 57, 109.

CON POULOS
Page 92.

TOBY SCOTT
Page 105.

IAN WALLACE
Page 77.

KATE WHITTAKER
Page 126.

CLARE WINFIELD
Pages 114, 136.